Born in 1924 in rural Kerala, K. G. Subramanyan played a pivotal role in shaping India's artistic identity after Independence. Initially studying economics, his involvement in the freedom struggle led to his imprisonment and debarment from college. He then joined Kala Bhavana, Visva-Bharati University, Santiniketan, which proved to be an enduring association. Graduating in 1948, he worked under such luminaries as Benode Behari Mukherjee, Nandalal Bose and Ramkinkar Baij. Subramanyan then taught at M. S. University, Baroda, and returned to his alma mater in Santiniketan as a professor in 1980.

Mani-da, as he was fondly called, seamlessly blended the elements of modernism with folk expression in his works that spanned paintings, murals, sculptures, prints, set designs and toys. His visual meditations contemplated human subjects and objects as distinct forms, characterized by vibrant colours and abstract shapes. Renowned for the sensuality in his imagery, reflective faces and nightly backdrops, his paintings reflected a cubist influence. Subramanyan skilfully blended romanticism with wit and eroticism, drawing inspiration from myth, memory and tradition. Beyond his visual artistry, his writings have laid a solid foundation for understanding the demands of art on the individual.

Spanning nearly seven decades, Subramanyan's art was featured in over fifty solo exhibitions, receiving prestigious awards such as the Medallion of Honourable Mention (Sao Paulo Biennale, Brazil) and the Lalit Kala Akademi's National Award. In 2012, he received the Padma Vibhushan, India's second-highest civilian award, for his outstanding contribution to the arts. He remained dedicated to teaching until his retirement in 1989, following which he was appointed as a professor emeritus at Visva-Bharati.

In the later stages of his life, Subramanyan lived with his daughter in Baroda, where he passed away in 2016 at the age of 92. His contributions have left an indelible mark on contemporary art, blending tradition with innovation.

BIRTH CENTENARY EDITION

ALSO AVAILABLE

Cat's Night and Day

Death in Eden

How Hanu Became Hanuman

How Poppy Grew Happy

In the Zoo

The King and the Little Man

Our Friends, the Ogres

Robby

The Tale of the Talking Face

When God First Made Animals, He Made Them All Alike

A Summer Story

Enchantment and Engagement
The Murals of K. G. Subramanyan
By R. Siva Kumar

Letters

The Living Tradition
Perspectives on Modern Indian Art

The Magic of Making
Essays on Art and Culture

Moving Focus
Essays on Indian Art

Poems

Seventy-Three

Sketches Scribbles Drawings

K. G. SUBRAMANYAN

Poems

LONDON NEW YORK CALCUTTA

Seagull Books, 2024

The poems collected in this book were first published in volume form by Seagull Books as *Poems* (2006) and *Poems: Rhymes of Recall* (2014).

© Seagull Books, 2024

ISBN 978 1 80309 457 1

British Library Cataloguing-in-Publication Data
A catalogue record for this book is available from the British Library

Typeset and designed by Seagull Books, Calcutta, India
Printed and bound by Hyam Enterprises, Calcutta, India

Contents

POEMS (2006)

Summer Noon	3
In the Night's Deep Furrow	4
The New Encounter	6
Nissim Revisited	7
Night Fall	8
Afternoon in August	9
Seaside Reverie	12
Cloud Time in Kailas	14
A Walk-back in Time	17
Resizing Each Other	21
The Seminar	28
The Photograph	31
Thoughts at Sundown	33
Neighbour	35
Then and Now	38
The First of Ashad	41
Gujarat 2002	46

Talking to Oneself with One's Ears to the Grass	50
Love at First Sight (Or Was It Second?)	56
The Conference	65
Farm Birds and Faces	69
The Odalisque and the Jumping Cat	72
The Pool	75
The Visitor	82
Odd Encounter	85
The Mirror	86
The Circle	87
The Annunciation	93
Purvapalli Sonnets	97
Renu-di	115
Demai-da	117
Dinner at Night	119
Viva Kundera	124
The Party	126
When You Close Your Eyes	132
A Long-lost Summer	133
Rain-soaked Evening	134
Doctor	135

POEMS: RHYMES OF RECALL (2014)

Recall	139
The First Encounter	141
On a Rainy Day	144
Reaching Out	146
The Health Walk	148
Wednesday Outing	153
Missed Tryst	157
Sense of Truth	158
The Riddle	163
Art and Artifice	167
Change of Weather	170
Monsoon Thoughts	172
The Wall	176
A Near Vision	179
Magic of Mantras	181
The Myna of Mynamati	183
Change of Scene	186
Reminiscence	188
Passage	190
After Malegaon	191
Homopolis	193

Speaking of Old Days	196
The Shadow	197
The Night at Rishikesh	199
To Somnath Zutshi	201
Shadow World	203

Poems (2006)

SUMMER NOON

It is like a forest of many suns
this summer noon.

Everyside one's shadow falls
It is nibbled away
By a counter-shining sun
At once.

I wonder whether there can be
substance without shadow.
Shadow-bare
Ghost-like
I move light-impelled
Between one orb of light and another.

This is ego-slaughter.

Almost as if the balls played the player.

IN THE NIGHT'S DEEP FURROW

In the night's deep furrow
Between two lidded leaves of sleep
Like a night-lily opening on the waters.

It is as if all one's likes had joined in one person
The bracing breaths of air
The coloured orbs of vision
The trees and landscape wrapped in
The sky's blue foil
The throbbing of the inner row of senses
And drawn one in
Between two coagulated shadows
Two lobes of intermeshing mystery.

There is no movement
Just the thrill of pleasure
No action
Just the muted hide and seek
Of an image and its shadow
In indecisive lineament
Between two lidded leaves of sleep.

The day's light then cuts dead open
All life's mystery
Sharpens the contours and shrinks the inner core

Cuts each limb adrift in autonomous action
The eye sees without knowing
The ear hears without feeling
The body acts without the inner push.
And the wish-bud sears within its slender stem.
The lazy acts roll out
Like listless coins
From a mechanical mint.

THE NEW ENCOUNTER

When you get on in years
And the body's fire runs cold
And in the heart's hammock lies
An aching emptiness

The sunbeams tip with gold
The sockets of your eyes
And the garden flowers' laughter
Goes tinkling in your ears

And in the vision of the world
Crowded with bird and beast
You see your wishes' flag unfurled
As in a holy feast.

It is like the mind has moulted
Cast off its crackled skin
And a bodiless body stepped out
From the wizened bones within
And hurtled through the wall of flesh

Into the heart of things
The grass's green, the rose's red
The earth's warm brown, the eyeless winds
The open blues of the endless skies
And those little dramas of birds and beasts
Or the nameless humans in the streets.

NISSIM REVISITED

It is not too bad
But it is not too good either
This poetry where you string words of daily speech
In loose locution.

You do get something out of them
Like a peek into the past
Or a tickle in the folds of memory
Bringing the common things that lie close to your skin
Closer to your skin.

But you feel you are in a familiar bed
Slept many times over
Wrapt in the same sweat and stains
The same blue drools of dreams
With the smell of amber and salt.

It does not amount to much
Just turns you side to side
In the same old common sleep.

What you need is a change of bed
That will jolt you into waking
Run a rake in your sodden chest
And tear its soil up.

And bring to green ignition
The heart's ceramic seed.

NIGHT FALL

Between the acid air
And the abrasive sea
The wrinkled rocks stand bare
In brown tenacity.

Adams flinty loins? Dadhichi's bones?
The time-scarred relics of a lifelong past
With latent fire within?
Or just dead stones?

The waves withdraw and slurp around their feet
The shadows thicken; the sea-birds drop their wing.
The temple noises from beyond the trees
Have an eerie ring.

Night falls like mist, black layer upon black layer.
The rocks, the sea, the sands, the sinking trees
Get pressed in a breathless mass
Between the earth and sky

Will the world outlast this night?
Will I break free?
Or lie sleep-stung to all eternity
A fly in fossil-stone?

AFTERNOON IN AUGUST

August.
The leaves in the garden sweat
And hang heavy with green.

In-between
The spiders weave their webs
And trap the sun-burnt hours.

That is when your skull cracks open
Like an over-grown fruit
To bare its inner burden
Blanched seeds of memory, pink seeds of dream
Wrapped in the sweet-stale smell
Of longings, hopes and fears.

A phantom floats in and whispers liplessly,
Do you remember?
Those days when the sky was blue
And the steaming sea-waves rolled on the fleshy sands
Filling its folds and fissures?

And the little crabs scurried in slanting lines in voiceless
    celebration?
And your soul ran naked against a viewless breeze?

Viewless but warm, fragrant with briar rose
And the jasmine buds in the folds of your mother's hair?

A long time has passed,
That smell is a washed-out dream.
The soul is wrapped with skins of circumstance
Now thin, now thick, stopping the breeze without.

Elders, well-wishers, friends
Fill you with common sense
Be tough, my boy; there are countless things to do.
The wind is a siren; will surely wear you down.
Keep yourself covered from its crazing touch.
They set you tasks, pump you with sound advice;
Show you the steps to climb, the paths to hurry through,
Hurdles to clear. Then show you the shining goals.
The waving hands. The name and the adulation.
The strings of smiles, the hugs, fans and friends.
The photo-features in the evening press.

Bravo! My boy, they say when these come to be,
In vicarious glee.

But in the deep within
Your soul has gone to sleep.
Deep dreamless sleep, dead to the wind without;
The sea, the sand, the crabs, the spiralled shells,
The shadows clinging to the feet of rocks.

But for a sudden whiff
Of the smell of your mother's hair
And a nagging ache
That whispers in your ear:
Will you let this be?
Won't you break free and breast the breeze again?
Before your idle soul
Becomes a witless hole?

SEASIDE REVERIE

On the western sky sail watercolour clouds.
The rude winds rock the heads of coconut palms
With rough spasmodic gusts.
The long-limbed shadows braid the warm with cool.

Below the road a bed of cream-white sands
And a crowd of rocks that look like pachyderms,
Wrinkled-round with rough-smooth sea-washed sides.
The roar of waves and the smell of salty air.

Crabs with lantern eyes and gawky legs
That run zig-zag with light and fluid step
Into the water, then retreat to little holes
That the backing waves sand-plug and seal with brine.

The jelly fish strewn on the steamy shore
Like lumps of limpid glass.
The washed-out shells, striped, mottled, horned and ribbed,
Grey mussels on the pitted side of rocks,
Sharp barnacles on the bottoms of the boats.

Then the monstrous waves maddened by unseen winds
Whipping the white shore with their foaming hoods,
The sea-birds whirling in the fog-bound sky
Within a screen of intermeshing cries.

The sea is a charmer, which with endless zest
Pipes out the snake of longing from your chest
Making you wish to go beyond its waves
And cross the line they touch the distant sky
To an unseen world beyond.
Which the sailboats sink to reach, sun sets to chase,
New lands, new habitations, new people, speech.

This is surprising. All thoughts of strange encounters
Makes me quake and coil up within.
Shelters my eyes and ears, weakens my knees
My neighbours snigger. A line of wicked girls
Burst into giggles when they see me blush
Under their stares.

But this crazy sea
Breaks down my barriers and sets me free.

CLOUD TIME IN KAILAS

There are certain days when death visits our house;
When the lizards roll their eyes and behave queer,
Rush behind the doors and click their tongues
In endless repetition like machines gone astray;
When the wall clock tick-tocks loud as if to say
Your time is running out.

Then the shadows swell and spread;
Grow hands and feet or horns and hairy tails;
Clamber on walls or crawl across the floor;
And tease the lights as a black cat teases mice
Frozen with fear.
Or lengthen out and leap from spot to spot;
Spill round the edges of the streets and chairs
Trickle to corners and then thicken there

Death has a special smell.
A mix of smoke, then camphor, mastic, musk.
It muddles your head and excavates your limbs
And reduces you to a wispy, weightless sheath.

These are some signs through which one's body feels
Its soft intrusion. There is no other proof.
I have had no chance to see death face to face.

They say you can't; he is sure to block your sight
Before he rides in on his buffalo,
Black like the monsoon clouds.
Red eyed, white-fanged he is himself midnight black
Only his hatchet is of shining steel.
And in one hand he holds a golden rope
With which he lassoes down your anima
Or what you call your spirit or your soul.

Some say that he has changed his methods now.
Altered his costume, even his instruments
They say he rides these days a black sedan
Steps down in a three-piece suit of blue and black;
Wears black shoes, black gloves and black head gear.
Carries no weapons, just words of courtesy.
Through a face, featureless, he whispers low:
Unpack, my friend. Come, put away your things.
Discard this wasted body. Erase your name.
And enter my van in full vacuity.
It is an easy drive from here to your real home;
You could even say it is instantaneous.
Your sojourn here was just a holiday.

But others say all this is fairytale.
When the body loses fight and lays down arms
The microbes take over; then the viruses.
More visibly the wriggly worms and maggots.
This is Nature's usual game.

It raises you from flesh; then wires you up;
Seeds you with ego, senses, power to think,
Stand separate and act with defiance.
Then breaks you down; brings you back to flesh
Feeds it to vermin: who eat and defecate
And leave you a roll of earth on common earth.

But this blue-black feeling and its bizarre trail of thought
Vanishes when a shaft of evening light
Enters the room in a burst of singing gold;
Scissors the shadows, sets free the captive lights.
Then the air awakens with the smell of kamini.
And the jarul stands floodlit with lilac flowers.

A WALK-BACK IN TIME

You sit at the window
And see the sunset's glow
Tinting the shiny roofs that slope towards the sea
And breaking the sombre shadows that lurk below
With sudden streaks of foam
Changing from pallid pink to deep incarnadine

Then the eye turns in.
And the mind starts moving in a time-lost land,
Once known now nameless, real but undefined.
With trees of forlorn visage, wind-blown plants
And paths that open forward and close behind
Step to unforeseen step.

Then it clambers down a pathless slope
Of greying earth and grass and turns abruptly left,
Then right, then round the bend, then through the cleft
In steep sandbanks towards a narrow road
That slowly struggles up to sunburnt streets
Hemstitched with shadows, filled with phantom forms
And sounds that float again the sunken barque
Of old reminiscence.

Little scenes of childhood.
The silver path that led you to the river

Where Mona held you hard between her thighs
And kissed you on the mouth. The sharp bird cries
That tore the air to shreds. The bramble wood
You chased the pheasants through;
The flowering bush freckled with butterflies
That flapped their wings and gave you oblique hints
Come catch us now, and let themselves be caught.
The flood of tears that wore your eyes down flat
When you chipped a careless wing.

The night with brown moths crawling on the wall
With wings like aged parchment marked with signs.
Curves, dashes, dots and strangely garbled rings.
The bony head and body thin as sheet
Of grandma on the mat on the mudwashed floor.
She died that night. The wailing and the vigil.
The smell of oil lamps. Eyes at the door.
And whispers hissing through the mournful dark.

The fateful letter that cut your life adrift.
Dad died in the garden while dozing in his chair;
Mum collapsed while walking down the stairs.
Within one week. You were not there.
And when you got the news it was late for tears.

You went home nevertheless, to a house shadowed with grief.
The floors were swept and the chairs were put around.
Friends came and sat, consoled and gave advice.
Some were free with words, others were brief.

But they all said the same. 'Be brave, my dears;
There is no person who can live forever;
The dead don't come back, the living have to live.'
So on and on, We could not stand it all.
Bee wore a mask and passed the tea around.
Then wept against the wall.

You got busy with work. Met Mat one day.
On the village road. And you became friends.
Then you met Jay at the tea shop and through him
The others in the mess. Hach tried his way
To make a living. Some traded odds and ends
Some worked in nearby towns. In the lamplight dim
Each evening you sat and discussed what was wrong
With the world that was. Then hatched every night
Little conspiracies to build it new.
You were not long together. Each went his way.
And you spent your time wandering in the woods.

Till one day you met Sue
Under the deep sky blue,
When one brilliant afternoon she walked her way
And you walked yours; and your pathways crossed.
Her wide astonished eyes seemed another sky
You could spread your wings across.
Then you walked again. And so did she
Till one fine day you found her hand in yours
And felt you had something to hold on to.

Wistful afternoons under jamun trees
Whose green leaves shone like silk
And threw green shadows on Sue's almond eyes
Wordless vows sitting in the river bed
Where the water brought the message skin to skin.

When sunset painted the grey horizon red
You both still felt not enough had been said.

That was all long ago.
Did the doorbell ring?

RESIZING EACH OTHER

They look at each other
And read each other's face
Like they were rolls of abstruse hieroglyphs.

Are his eyes too watery?
Is her mouth aslant, cheeks puffed or pleated down?
His swollen eyelids are they a shade too brown
And pouchy down below?

Is her breathing heavy? Her colour a trifle wan?
Is that his head that seems a copper pan
Through strands of thinning hair?

She sees him on the sly; he watches her
When she is inattentive. But when their eyes
Cross each other they break into a laugh.

Each doubtless knows what the other one is thinking
More or less. They are taking stock
Of life's wear and tear. Afraid silently

Of what is yet to be; wondering whether
They can work the miracle of walking together
Into the shaded woods.

That is not simple; no, not any more
Unless they forced the door—
Like the Koestlers did many years ago.

Fifty years of restless hide and seek,
Sitting side by side, sharing the same bed,
Holding hands and being intimate
Watching the crescent moon
Sail on the star-strewn sky.
Walking the gravel path covered with shiuli flowers.
Or when the summer storm mauled the earth
Sitting locked in worry; but when it passed
Picking the fruit it shook down from the trees.
Inching in every act towards each other
To tear the viewless veil that hung between.

Did that tear the veil? It sometimes did.
But it closed up soon enough.

Again they started on the self-same search
This time on other lines.

Poking eyes with eyes to see something beyond,
Forcing the body's gates to reach some inner core,
Stripping each word and gesture to see its hidden truth,
Its confounding depths, eloquent vacancies
Its unspelt implications. But all this bore
Them back to themselves as through a mocking mirror

Enlarged, fragmented, twisted out of shape
Sometimes sharply drawn, sometimes a blur.

Maybe in-between
Behind the busy scene
They got some fleeting glimpses of each other's being
Beyond the usual frames and ego fields.
Not when they were locked in viewing each other,
Striving to woo and win or rip each other down
But lost sight of themselves in doing other things,
Becoming transparent.

Which made them see that the veil is within each
That puts to one the other out of reach.
You can't meet another without the ego's thrust
But you can't mix unless you lose it first.
To gain you have to lose. To see you have to look
The other way with free unfocussed eyes.
To stake the claim you have to lose your aim.

One isn't enough; to see what one is like
You need a second; but to see the second
You need the larger world. And in this
You need a staunch and seasoned accomplice.

So this witless craving to hold to each other
And the wish to cross even the gates of death
Still hand in hand.

But time does take its toll.

Their limbs are heavy now; their senses half asleep.
Their eyes don't lift and reach the vaulted skies
Nor bend and touch the earth below their feet
Like they did once.

It takes whole day and night
Just to size each other right

True, the mind has skies that are more spacious
Than the spaces we know of,
More planets, galaxies and stellar clouds.
And its spread is larger than our tinted vaults;
Its ground is wider than our arching globe.

So they often amble through its twisted paths
In the light of various times.
Pink light of childhood, the sanguine light of youth,
The late-life violet, the ageless blue,
Till they come upon those walls with graffiti
That brings back to them their past to some degree.

A windy evening in early March
Cloaked with a silver light
And sashed with palas flowers.

Sowing the earth with a kind of deep unease,
Spreading a fever in the brittle air.

They met at a little shop in the nearby town,
Where he bought cigars and she bought chocolate,
And lent him change when he was short for some.
He felt embarrassed. But she smiled and said
That he could lend her too when she needed some.

They walked back to campus on the starlit road
Wrapped in a web of warmth, but without words.

Till Vimal rode them down on his rattling bike
And unscrewed them both with his sense of garrulous fun
Making wild insinuations. Her face went red
And he was furious. But in the growing fuss
And altercation they met eye to eye
And became strangely shy.

Vimal left that summer. To see him off
They went to the railway station and waved and waved
Till the train was lost to view. And each one thought
What an angel Vimal was while on their way.

Vimal became an angel soon enough.

A taxi knocked him down on a Bombay street
Where he went to seek a job.
That ended his job on earth. But they both felt
That he will still be there in the wind and weather
Bringing people together.

This mishap stressed their need for each other.
So they rushed to wed.
On a summer afternoon.
On an old friend's lawn and as it came to be
Between two plantain trees and a blazing fire.
Below the rainbow cloud of Vimal's gaze
That sailed in viewless from some outer space
Which they both saw but the others did not see.

The priest chanted mantras and explained what they meant
In his own fashion. Friends ate sweets,
Sipped scented sherbet, exchanged whispered notes.
There was soft music and the smell of incense sticks.
And the distant trees were loud with parakeets.

They were choked with smoke and fears of the yet to be
To read the restless message in each other's eye.
To the sitting crowd they looked like painted dolls
Put out on view; starched clothes and satin curls
And sewed on smiles and blank bewildered eyes.

Then came the time to be declared man and wife
Walking the seven steps around the fire,
And be pelted saffron-rice by well-wishers.

The night was hot. The stars were sharp and bright.
When the shehnai faded out and people left.

Too tired for dinner they drank just almond milk
Flavoured with khus. With jokes and pleasantries

They were dragged and pushed into a tiny room
Festooned with flowers; and made beautiful
In many ways. With paintings on the wall
And flowers in fancy pots. Provoking prints.

But standing eye to eye
Before the balcony
That night they wanted nothing else to see.
On their mind's moving screen little glimpses flash.

He was so comic but his eyes were warm.
His body was all bones but his lips were soft
Smelling of cigars and the camphor of desire,
She blushed to think.
She was so clumsy, he recalled with a smile,
In hiding what she had she revealed all.

The fire-flies flew in loops above their head
Writing a message all too plainly said.

The night was crazy. Between the scented sheets
She counted all the bones she could lay hands on.
And he read her with his touch like a page in braille.
Line by secret line. In the woods of night
Between the moss of sleep and the mist of dreams
They flowed like wayward streams
Meeting and mingling till they hurtled down
In a thundering cascade amidst the marble rocks.

THE SEMINAR

The seminar was delightful. The girls were pretty.
Even when they chewed the skins of the new art-speak
Between their teeth.

The boys were witty
And said outrageous things in the guise of tongue-in-cheek
Then stifled a squeak of laughter in their throats.

Damn art and artists, theory is our forte.

Then came stories of how art came to be.
The pre-phase, the post-phase, the hazy interlude.
Some cited Marx, some quoted Mallarmé,
Some spat upon the past and said things rude
Mixing style with bile, history with fairytale.
Then the endless personal angle,
The itch in the loins, the pain in the heart,
The ceaseless confrontations in the head.

The angst, the anger. And the waverings.
To be or not to be? To do or die?
Stand up and fight or just go to bed
With teasing hopes and tantalizing dreams?

They compared notes about its present state
While munching the mutton tikkis on their plate.

There were slogans too, scripted on boards and cloth.
Live in the present, leave your grandma's lap.
Switch off romantic twilight. Cut the crap
Of ageless wisdom. What is new is true.
Hold hands with gays, they also live and love.
Save brides from burning, catch and geld the grooms.
Don't stand in fear, art should interfere.
Don't foul the walls, it is better to instal.
So on and on and it all sounded good.

The tea was excellent and the pastries soft
While they waved and gestured and held the flags aloft

The slides, too, were revealing frame to frame.
A black man lowers over a yielding white.
A brown man breaks his walls to peek out West
Or paints them red inside to pep himself.
The red star transforms into a yellow heart
Padded smooth and swollen like a tart.
Macabre masks. Bodies with painted scars
In dark ox-blood. Rituals out of site
Or time. Without a purpose or the inner bite.
Just loud, exotic, ethnic sound and mime
To regale wrinkled grannies and sniggering boys
In Rockefeller Plaza or Hampstead Heath.

You are all there and yet you feel so far.
Like watching fish across a wall of glass
In cool aquaria. The coloured gills and scales,

The streaming tails, intriguing pouts and stares,
Quick climbs and dips and dives in breathless grace.
But in drip-fed water over hand-picked rocks.
And cultivated plants. And controlled light.

It is another world.
But in the rhythmic gurgle of the water-drip
And the rising stream of bubbles, a random word
Picks you in its beak like a wild sea-bird
And takes you somewhere else.
Through various passages of graded black

To a gate of open light.
Beyond which lies
A lengthy landscape of undulating green
Waving with white kash flowers.

A small girl runs up and clambers on your lap
Folds you in her arms and whispers soft,
I am Cinderella of the crystal shoes
Who comes to be when all words burn to ash.
I shan't stay long for the magic does not last.
You bend forward to kiss her on the hair.
When Dona Philips breaks the little trance,
Sorry dear. I have to go out now,
The pepper soup won't let me sit in peace.

So you got something from this exercise.
It made you wakeful if not very wise.

THE PHOTOGRAPH

My Pa was short, much shorter than my Ma.
She was five-foot six. He was just five-foot-one.
But he looked substantial, almost like solid rock.
For all her height my Ma looked very slight,
Like a splash of ocean spray that broke on it.

Ma had a moist grey look in her eyes
When they swam across the air to look at you.
They came and caressed you. Their silken touch
Draped your shoulders with a silver glow.

Pa was muscular, well-built and bound.
Looked almost like a nimble samurai,
His every limb tattooed with watchfulness.
But his eyes had all the time a tiny twitch.
And having lost his hair in early life
His head was bald, which every fifteen days
A barber came and shaved and shined again.

Ma's ears were long,
Made longer by two massive ear-plugs.
Gold chased on lac, that she wore all the time.
But there were times she put on other things,
(When someone called or there was a feast at home).
Ringlets of gold edging her yellow lobes,

A choker of beads and pearls. Long necklaces
That carried rows of mohurs, tiger claws.
Bangles from wrist to elbow. Armlets with beads.
A snaky waist-band. Anklets with bells.
Toe-rings shaped like loops of scorpions.
With all these, she outshone her wrinkled age
And looked like a haloed icon in a shrine.

She wore them last when they took this photograph,
When she forced my Pa to wear a gold-edged turban
And a pleated shawl across his brawny chest.
Then placed me in-between
I had black eyes and unpressed shirts and shorts
And feet that ached in polished leather shoes.

Soon after this,
She sold these one by one to run the house.
Barring a locket on a yellow string
And those ear-plugs that flanked her benign face.

There is not much left in the photograph,
The image has faded, leaving a yellow-smudge.
What I see now is in my mind's recall.

THOUGHTS AT SUNDOWN

From where you sit you see the sun go down
Orange, red, then slowly purple, brown.
The day was hot. So it is great relief;
Night will be balm to your swollen sun-baked eyes.
But when it was cold you wanted the sun to stay
And fire your frigid nerves both night and day.

The bush is spangled with red hibiscus.
The tree behind has a veil of creamy flowers
Like a dressed-up bride.
The leaves that drooped at noon now raise their heads.

There are whispers in the air, nibbling the ears
And nudging to life the repressed dreams within.
Then the plaintive noises. The crow-chicks' throaty caws.
The restless call of koels.
The sound of distant trains.
Puffing soft but loud beneath the bridge.

Trains no more whistle. They low like buffalos
This skips the ears and hits somewhere below,
Raising a wish within your surprised ribs
To go somewhere.

But where?
Your legs are wooden now.

The hips are stiff; knees wobble when you stand.
With every move the head goes in a whirl.
The body is now baggage;
It no more carries you,
You have to lug it round.
So the only choice there is,
Is to leave it where it is
And forge freely ahead.

This makes you wonder, will you still be there
When you have left it back?

Some say, yes.
They show you cards showing what you will be,
In curious geometry.
Then unroll maps engraved in many colours
Of worlds you can journey to.

The others laugh and say, Are you off your nut?
Without the flagon what will the spirit hold?

But it is good to think
That you will still be there;
A bodiless body in airy nakedness
Weightless but wakeful,
Floating in open skies in gay abandon.

Did you say gay?
Yes, gay, you smile and say,
For in that state we shall be all one kind.

NEIGHBOUR

He turns up now and then.
But these days rarely.

He is leaner now. His cheeks are hanging loose,
His eyes are sunk in shadows. His loud voice
Is stuck deep in his throat,
To let out which his mouth has to open wide.

Today he has his black bitch on a leash.
Cool quiet thing; covered with limp black hair.
Has mind-melting eyes. She is now twelve, he says.
Looks well for her age, I mumble.
He nods with satisfaction. Adds, sleeps all the time.
That is natural, I say; were she a human being
She would be ninety now,
Sunk in a bed or stuck in a grey wheelchair.

He sits on the sofa chair.
Crosses his leg.
Then with every breath
Crosses the left on right, the right on left.
This is compulsive
It puts his mind at ease.

Till finally, he pulls out a cigarette
Lights it up and fills his mouth with smoke.

Then throat and lungs and nasal passages.
This alters the focus of his fidgeting.
He sneezes, coughs and wipes his mouth and nose.
But the legs have now some rest.

I sit back and watch.
And start wondering
Where does my voice sit when I start to speak?
Inside the throat? Or cheek? Or on the tongue?
Is it stentorian or a petty squeak?
And when I visit others and sit on their chairs
Do I crack my knuckles,
Or dance my feet
To put my mind at ease?

He is busy now, he says, writing some verse;
His wife is on vacation in the hills,
Novels, he can't write. They need locations
And people of flesh and blood, say the publishers.

His characters don't belong anywhere.
They are bodiless. They walk with toeless feet.
They kiss with lipless mouths.
They talk with wordless whispers.
Or toneless gutturals.

It can't be otherwise, he confesses.
He grew up rootless in a foreign land
Between dream-timing tribals

And pragmatic whites
Both rather out of reach.

That is strange I say;
We reach out to birds;
We befriend animals both tame and wild;
Even lizards on the wall, toads on the floor.

Sure, we do, he says.
But men are different. They carry a world with them.
Forests, deserts, mountains, lakes and seas,
All fringed with coloured skies. Even walled cities
With many gates, intriguing passages,
Cobbled with light and shadow.

They are never there by themselves;
Each has around a special entourage.
So floats aloof like a separate island
Walled by roaring breakers you can't cross.
Unless you have a hard-earned strategy.

The bitch now barks. And he gets up to go.

She wants her evening walk, he smiles and says,
All day she sleeps, but this
She will never miss.

THEN AND NOW

Nothing remains the same.

This was a wilderness when you came here first
Though not a howling desert or a woodland thick with trees,
Just a place that met the sky in privacy.
Far from the crowd of men.

A pebbly piece of earth,
Washed bare by winds in summer, by water in the rains.
Where grasses grew tall,
And the sturdy palmyras with fan-shaped leaves.
And all the rest was small.

The lanky date-palms notch-cut at the neck
Like crazy punks, with a crown of spiky leaves.
Stunted mango trees; sour-plum bush.
Thorned simul trees with crimson cup-like flowers
Standing like candelabra;
Crowded with raucous birds.
Thin palas, whose blossoms burned like fire
In cool-black chalices that lined their stems.
The seven-leafed mascot tree
That tempted the patron to make this settlement,
And gained its special status.
Then clumps of bamboo round the scattered huts
That went wild in a storm and swayed their heads
Like soothsayers in a trance.

Each was special
But they did not stand together
To make an impression.
Like those in the tourist sites;
Grouped, groomed and ordered by landscape architects.
Flattered by artists in their watercolours.
And reproduced in posters on the walls.

Yet they had each
A special kind of speech
That called you close and whispered shamelessly,
See me for myself. Come and read my name
In the crinkles of my skin,
My knots and crevices,
The folds of my leaves and the funnels of my flowers,
My fruits and pods with flat uncloven seeds.

You spent four years to make their acquaintance;
Hearing their murmurs; sniffing their gummy sap,
Reading the stories scripted on their trunks;
Getting a thrill from the touch of their leaves and flowers
Aping their awkward gestures. Desperate
To fill your work with these.

But that was hard to do. The most you got
Was a smudgy fingerprint.

But even that was rewarding as it went.
You can't have it all.

Did not some thinker say
That all this art is but a shadow-play?

When I had to leave I left with a heavy heart.
With a curious feeling just below the ribs
That brought me close to tears.
I mooned around each site, each tree and bush
Of this world I knew for many days on end.

Their images survive.
For now and then, when I try to call them back
They step out just as they were in those days
Lean, ascetic, bony, intimate
Dated spectres from a world that was.
Certainly strange to the people of today.

For their recent successors are fat and lush;
And in a crowd, not single, separate.
Each shooting higher to catch the sun's first rays
In jostling competition. They have lost
Their old proportions, even characters.
More artful now, they are less articulate.

They do not excite me as their parents did.
Maybe my eyes have lost their appetite,
And hold to what they knew when they were keen.
This is but natural. It is hard for one
Used to the slender beauties of the Book of Hours
To fall to the charms of the bulgy denizens
Of the fleshy world of Peter Paul Rubens.

THE FIRST OF ASHAD

The morning is murky.
Above, the sodden sky
Clay-washed with clouds.
Below a faceless earth
Swaddled in grey.

My eyes are bleary.
The head is half asleep.
So, turn on the radio while sipping tea.

That makes it worse.
It comes with long reports
Of gangrapes, massacres.
Of a king and queen shot by their son and heir
In a drunken frenzy.
Of children sold like chicks
By those that bore them
For a wad of foreign money.

Then a pause. A purring sound. A noisy ad.

On summer days when your body comes to boil
Dab your head with fragrant Brahmi oil.

More news from far on the yawning TV set.
Below a Dhyani Buddha

A madcap knifes to death a bunch of girls.
Frozen with fright the rest don't remonstrate.
Before the eyes of a compassionate Christ
A rootless youth shoots down a dozen boys,
With an automatic rifle.
The dead are not discussed.
What is discussed is the right to own a gun
And the hallowed privilege
To shoot each other in free democracy.

Nearer home, to please a mother goddess
A peasant slays his son, to earn the boon
Of endless manhood.
In a cosy curtained cell,
To the sound of pipes and drums,
A goodman shows the gates of Paradise
To a bunch of boys and girls in his Brindaban,
But the police get the scent.
And nab him in the act.

They talked of a new millennium for days on end
Only a year ago.
Foresaw a change of scene. But this is how
A morning starts today.

Clouds no more carry the coloured messages
Of pining lovers across a rain-soaked land
Over rolling hills covered with shiny grass,
Fields ploughed for sowing, bright and festive towns,
Like they did once in the time of Kalidas.

Instead a roll of beeps. To follow, rumbling sounds
Or a gasp of silence. Before things move again
With a prolonged whine.
Starts News Magazine.

Bush talks of NATO; he was there with open arms
To hug Europe to peace. He says with emphasis,
Europe was one and it shall so remain.
Forget the two wars of those twenty years
Followed by sixty of growls and posturings,
They won't return. For with our force of arms
We shall wipe outright such possibility.

The posters scream below his smiling face
Stand with the NATO and be tension free.

But we shall nurse your old diversities,
In dress, in tongue, in ways you live and love.
By gad, we shall. They are the salt of life,
You can have your orgies and your tournaments,
You can squabble freely in your parliament,
Or on the sporting fields. Or Olympics.
And we shall pay for it.

They are essential in a live democracy.
And those peppered stories on the NBC.

Then he sniggers at his joke.
And quickly downs a Coke.

The people smirk and clap. And dream of dollar loans.
Or grants and other sops that come with these.

This was in Kosovo. Now to Vatican.

In a columned church floodlit with candlelight
An aged pope bent low with robe and crown
Makes saints of those who performed miracles.
He mumbles, Now mercy is not enough;
Devoid of magic, kindness can't convert.

A short commercial selling foreign soap.

Then comes our minister with a beaming smile.
Talks of the march of time.
The road we left behind, the road ahead
That will lead us forward to that rainbow land
We always aspired for.
If we persevere. And lay aside our doubts
About the scraps the others dump on us.
Though fetid wastes of their erstwhile affluence
They will fertilize our growth:
Some will serve our needs; others will not
But that is in the game.
Some may be harmful, others innocent;
But that is natural,
Good comes with bad.

The audience snoozes. But asks for incentives.
For a few rupees they will accept anything.

Then a clap of thunder.
To follow, a heavy shower,
Then a headlong wind that sweeps it through the window
And swamps the cement floor.

They have switched off the current, the central supply men.
To avoid any catastrophe,
If a wire breaks loose or a tower comes crashing down.
Foresight is better, they make sure to say,
Than tardy hindsight after the harm is done.

This shuts out the world the media brought to you.
And you sit alone
In the daylight dark as night,
Or nearly so.
And think of the things you heard, the things you saw.
Their implications. Their where and when and why.

Then question yourself—
For all the virtues of our mind and muscle
Has ten millennia made us better men?

GUJARAT 2002

Mantras, mandalas,
Magic words and chants;
Mystic signs and microcosmic charts.

To give form to something that is beyond form,
To say in words what is beyond all saying,
Or pin at a point what is everywhere.

Gods of many kinds you can adore,
Cradle in your arms or enthrone high
In a reachless empyrean in the sky.

Tantalizing ploys. Bright decoys
To get you out of yourself; shed the skin
Of ego that keeps you firmly bound
To thoughts of your *existence*, not your *being*.

When you are born you have a living eye,
Keen ears and touch that feel and unmask things.
And tongue that fashions words to encode them.

Then your heart glows green.
Your head is a raging forge.

But as time goes by they lose their wakefulness.
The green grows grey; the forge is choked with ash

The eyelids droop, the tongue grows fat and stiff.
Ears miss the sound of the inner voice of things,
Your actions answer only your little needs.
To sell. Feel safe. Succeed. Or overcome.
They don't go beyond.

This starves your heart. And fills your empty head
With a monstrous wish to line against its walls
These ideas and tools as ultimates.

Blowing them up. Giving them personae.
Painting eyes on some; giving some open mouths
With shining smiles or saw-toothed grimaces.
Granting them arms and legs and features wild.
Rigging them up with clothes and weaponry.

Those who won't idolize wrap them with words
That turn and twist into tangled mysteries
That each one interprets to suit his ends.

So what was designed to lead you to your being
Now stands out as a fortress outside it.
With vaults lit by a row of crazy dreams,
For ego sports and empty indulgence.
Feeding your greed. Deepening your fears.
Estranging you from your essential goals.

There are no ways now.
There are only walls.
Dividing each from each.

Which move around to raise a maze of shrines,
With domes and minarets. Steeples and towers.
Temples. Churches. Synagogues. And mosques.
Managed by mullahs, pandas, rabbis, priests.
Or their hangers-on. Their bank-men and their clerks.
Armies and ad-men; who,
To keep in business,
Devise novel confrontations
Under the deceiving cover
Of feasts, parades, Ids, anniversaries.
With bright displays and loud brainbashing sounds,
Mindless orgies. Witless delivery.

Coarsened by these,
Men lose their feel for others
Are deaf to the advice of their inner being.
And blind to what will be.

They run amok,
They kill without compunction.
They burn people alive,
Dishonour girls, put babies to the sword,
Without any sense of guilt.

They do all this because
They chose to erect walls
Where they should have fashioned ways
To that inner space
Where they all could feel the same.

And forgot the sage advice
Of an unusual man
Who for thirty years
Led their morning prayers
With Narsi Bhagat's hymn
That started with the line—

Friends, they alone are pious
Who feel another's pain.

TALKING TO ONESELF WITH ONE'S EARS TO THE GRASS

I lie and lay my head upon the grass
And unwind the body hardened stiff like glass,
But the tiny blades tickle the lower ear
Making me ask myself, why do I bear
This crass impertinence and sink my head
Still further down its bed of prickly green?

To hear the pulse-beat of the labouring earth?
The movements of the life it holds within?
Its cries of passion? Its groans of pain?
The secret struggles in its inner veins?
The worms that chew its soil, the tunnelling rats,
Crickets that chirp with shivering leg and wing?
The flipping open of the fat seed pods
To let the sprouts emerge?
The rustling flurry of the flying ants?

I am not sure.

But I have learnt by this

That the earth is not as silent as we think
It has as many sounds as has a crowded street.
Horns, hoots, explosions, shouts, sirens, shrieks;
Rounds of raucous speech.

Its traffic is no lighter,
Though the sound levels are low;
Heard from near just modest symphonies.
But amplified, their roar can burst your ears.

Where did I hear or read,
That in the world somewhere
They have built a library
Of sounds of various kinds?
Not just the songs and speech of human beings
Or the music made with diverse instruments.
But a larger collection.
Of noises from roads and woods,
From mills and factories,
Machines of locomotion.
Currents of wind and weather.

Even body sounds that fill a stethoscope
And tell our doctors what is wrong with us.
The pounding of the pulse. The pace of the heart.
The shameless rumblings in the intestines.
The gasps and spasms that plague the struggling lungs.
The sniffles and wheezes in the nose and throat
The total orchestra that plays in the pit
Below the tumult of the outside world.

This is truly crazy; nevertheless,
There is nothing here for us to wonder at.

For we live as much with sounds as we do sights.
Read them separate or link them up;
Get, through their help, a vision of the world.
Often they please and transfigure our moods.
Sometimes they weigh them down and depress us.

But those that affect us or carry meaning
All dwell within the backyard of our minds,
The raw young ones and the aged veterans,
Who link their limbs in shameless dalliance
When they get together. This is compulsive.

So, all those sounds that make some sense to us,
Move us deep or motivate our acts
Rise from this valley of their waywardness.

A new word chums up with an older one.
A new tune reaches out to an old refrain
Of fifty years ago.
Redraws the venue. Redoes the rhyme and rhythm.
A new piece of speech contacts an older one;
Alters its substance in its ancient light.
Or vice versa. They don't stand alone.

To think of it, where will the present be
If the erstwhile past denied to play its host?
And would we know the nature of our past
If the present failed to clothe its hazy ghost?

Besides, the sights we see and the sounds we hear
Are fed and mothered by our fantasy.
In the narrow space between its massive breasts
They grow and find a fecund universe.
(Even larger than the one the books describe)
Shifting their starting signs. And churning out
New constellations, comets, meteors;
Some shaped and sleek; some idiosyncratic.

So we talk about the music of the spheres.
Of voices in the viewless firmament,
Or the magic mantras of the Milky Way,
Between whose stations we can float or fly
Exploring new locations, latitudes,
Space-skiing, as it were, on slopes of sound.

But not forever.

The first excitement palls.
And the sounds that once surprised turn stale and false.
The songs grow shrill. The chantings sag and sigh.
The mantras moo like cows; bird cries bleat.
Losing their aim and logic they run astray
Become unruly, tear each other down,
Raising a mad commotion.
Which splits our ears and petrifies our head.
And makes us deaf to our own inner speech.

In the face of this we long for *soundlessness*.
Sticking our fingers in the sockets of our ears
We cry for *silence*.
For a zone of *soundless peace*.

A voice, then, whispers from inside our thought,
It is unlikely that you will find such peace.
If you insist on a fully soundless one.

For, when things came to be in the first instance,
Through a sudden bang or a chain of happenings,
Its force unrolled a subtle wave of sound
That entered everything.
This can't be quelled
Unless you kill it all.
(Which you cannot as a tiny part of it.)

But you can train your ears to bear its drone,
Which is low in tone, limited in register.
It is worth the effort; you won't regret it;
For its wavelength washes out all troubling noise
Or soaks it in. And below its muted vault
You will hear your inner speech quite loud and clear.
And what is silence but this clarity?

The voice is perhaps right. It is worth a try.
When you strain to see too much and the tired eyes
Bulge and blister with its excess load
Drain them out; and see a little less.

When your eager ears are over-stuffed with sounds
Don't fail to flush them out and clear the mess

You won't miss anything. You don't need it all.

The world has more things than a library can list;
Or museum hold in store.
The more our senses probe, mare things will come to light.
And not all these are designed for our needs
To discover ourselves, to live our lives in full,
Or face our ends with equanimity

Hasn't someone said,
Out of the waters of eternity
We can only scoop as much
As our little palms can hold?

Desire for more can only frustrate us.
We can't find all. And everything we find
We can't utilize. And this disturbs us.
Just look around the mess we live amidst.
Piles of pamphlets. Rows of books. Now tapes
Or CD-ROMS. The windows on the world.

Like the proverbial ass,
We moan (or bray), Alas!
When will we get through all this endless grass?

LOVE AT FIRST SIGHT
(OR WAS IT SECOND?)

When Shyam saw Sue on a cloudy afternoon
Along with Lee and Bee the only thing
He noticed was that she was rather short
Had a narrow head and slightly heavy jaws
And wore her hair like a wimple on her head
Flat and loose and rather lustreless.

And hid her body with a heavy shawl.

But he also saw two honey-coloured eyes
That flew like moths to wherever she looked.
Shyam felt uneasy; raised his hand and waved.
But felt a fool when Lee asked what it meant.
He smiled and said, Nothing. He surely knew
It was a feeling not a real thing.

That night his dreams were full of flying moths.
Streaked and spotted with various coloured marks.
They danced around the thicket of his sleep.
Was there a message in their wavy script?
A meaning in the whisper of their wings?
He was not sure, but had a busy night.

The morning next was full of things to do.
In the afternoon there was a seminar,
Which lasted hours; ended when lights came on.
It had its value. They talked on aesthetics.
Each one gave chase to those elusive things
That thronged the mind's thin air. Though none was
    caught
The exercise fuelled one's flagging thoughts.

When he hobbled back that night to this hostel room
Thinking of these and munching a late-night snack
He was very tired; and quickly went to sleep.

At the dead of night the birds were boisterous
Koels perhaps; they get their signals wrong.
Or were they curlews with their wailing calls?
Under the cloak of sleep he was not sure.
But the night was rife with sounds of many kinds
Which he floated on as on a crazy sea
Tossed up and down but close-eyed all the time.
This continued for hours, till finally,
When the clock struck eight and the sun had climbed the
    trees
The rice-mill's siren shook him out of bed.

He opened his eyes and raised them to the wall
As he always did, to know what time of day,
Good gracious! There on its sunlit field
Sat a honey-coloured moth with haunting eyes.

Was it a sign that he had hoped to see?
Or a warning from which he would rather flee?

That day the sun shone bright. The bamboo groves
Went wild with winds whistling a rousing tune
The mist-bound trees suddenly wandered out
Like girls in a fashion show. All clad in green.
But sashed with diverse colours. Sequinned with light.
What is afoot? Shyam sat and asked himself
A miracle? A new world moulting out
From the drab old one he had stopped to think about?

Sue woke up too, to notice such a change
Which made her do things she never did before

For once she scanned her face in the looking glass
And noticed there the signs of long neglect.
For once she asked herself with a sense of shame
Was her body given her to trifle with?

That afternoon she plaited her brown-black hair
And coiled the plaits on both sides of her head.
She wore white flowers in the fold of her shell shaped ears
A string of beads that slid between her breasts
And a weightless shawl that showed her body out.

Lee noticed it. As also Sue's profile.
With a quivering softness in the nose and lips.
Like those of girls one saw in the palace scenes
Of the album paintings in the Chamba hills.

And a laugh that showed two rows of pearly teeth.
And a tiny cloven chin shining beneath.

Heavens, what transformation? She told Shyam
He nodded, yes. His eyes had seen it too.

They met that evening in the Mango grove
Talked of the change in weather.
Though for Lee and Bee
It was the same as on the other days.

The same shameless sun; the dark and dowdy shad
The same mad winds that ruffled their modesty
The same scent of flowers that coarsened into stink

But for Shyam and Sue there was a distinct change
Looking eye to eye they spoke within their breath
How can they miss an open thing like this?

In the following days Shyam felt the morning breeze.
That rolled dry leaves and teased the tips of flowers,
Creep below his feet and lift him up
Level with tops of trees. Even clouds above.
And sun beams sneak into his sleepy eyes
And remove the film that fogged his normal gaze.

He noticed now what he never did before.

In whatever he saw, things big and small.
In each a grand design. An inborn liveliness.
An energy that spread from core to skin.
A magic in the air. Music in skies.
Mixing shape and colour, sound and touch and motion
Into complex metaphors.
That jumped the fence of each divided sense.

This made him think of Tagore's famous ode
The Waking Waterfall
Rock-locked, dream-frozen once;
But thawed to overflow
Life's endless variety. Smash all the sluice-gates
And flood the landscape of his hungry mind
For all the days to come.

Will this happen to him? Will something break
His opaque shell? Give him the open skies?

Not far away
Sue lay supine upon a wooden bed

Facing a ceiling framed with rainbow ribs
Recalling verses from the songs of *Sur*
Or Tulsi or Kabir.
Or sonnets of love composed by Jayadev
Where the body gained a hallowed existence,
Its inner cries the purity of prayer;

Its acts of passion a sense of sacrament.
The shining rhythms of whose narrative
Spread around a strange incandescence
Where the leafy bowers of a lover's nest
Seemed lofty arcades of a sacred shrine.

Why did she keep in harness all these years
This instrument that cross-linked heaven and earth,
Transforming both? See mischief in its lights?
Read madness in its beeps? Give foolish ears
To the dos and don'ts of those who misused it?

It was waking up today, this lovely beast.
Saying here I am to take you where you want.
Giving you legs or wings or paddling feet,
Or other means to go from place to place.

The thought of this brought to her face a laugh;
When Bee came and asked What are you dreaming of?

Was this because of a drastic change of air?
The end of rains? The advent of the fall?
The blue smile of sky that broke the veil of clouds
And rang cymbals in the hollows of your heart?

So it seemed to Shyam.
And also Sue.

Till Sue had to leave the campus for a while
To attend her sister's wedding in Lahore.

Shyam, Lee and Bee, all, went to see her off
To the railway station. Put her on the train.
Waved her away. Made no effort to speak.
Below their smiles there was a shade of pain;
They would miss her badly for an endless week.

To cover this feeling they romped back noisily
Hopping and running on the dusty road,
Seeming like frisky calves to passers-by.
It was some relief. At least to Lee and Bee.
It let them marvel at the sunset's glow,
Hear the homing birds. Smell the dew on earth.
But Shyam could only see a grey nightfall.

The next few days, things went from bad to worse;
Shyam's soaring spirits sank; his eager eyes
Refused to seek the things he loved to see;
And all those things that keyed his senses up
Lost their savour. And he walked around
With a hang-dog look. Which was seen by Lee and Bee.
Though first perplexed they came to, soon, guess why.
Raising their heads to the parchment of the sky
As if to read some sign it bore above
They said with gravity—*It looks like love.*

In her festive home, Sue felt a stranger too.
She could not ride the rising tide of fun
The wedding came up with. No, not this time.
The lights were jarring. The loud and joyful sounds
Of drums and pipes and the singing of the girls
Were tasteless to her ears. Her friends' explosive mirth
Seemed to her uncouth. Even her dear Lahore,
She always raved about, now seemed a bore.
This surprised her friends; they thought, each one,
What has switched off this girl so full of fun?

Her sister could surmise. As she had felt the same
When Inder was away. For two long years.
She whispered in their ears—*It seems like love.*

Sue came back sooner than she planned to do.

And when she did the lights went up again
For the group of four; but much more so for Shyam.
Life filled his landscape; colours swamped his skies.
He was certain now that he was hooked for good.
Only with Sue around he could regain
The things he thought were lost. Sue also came to see
That with Shyam around her eyes got back their wings,
Her ears their thrill, her mind its usual bounce.

The world had more to it when both were near.

This was a puzzling thing—To feel less than what you were
Till someone came and swept you off your feet
Then made you own the earth and hold the skies
In that rimless space between two pairs of eyes.
Enlarged the boundaries. Altered the beat.
Made the blood run wild. Hearts burn like stoves
It was wanton dependency. This thing called love.
This need to lose one's heart to gain the world.

Does this inhere in the body's chemistry?
Or something in the nature's reigning codes?

THE CONFERENCE

She went to Paris for a conference.
They had gathered there from all corners of the world
To discuss poverty.
Unfurled
Colourful banners on the streetside poles.
Put tiny flags before their numbered seats.
Pinned glowing badges on their overcoats.

Sadiq had drawn the paper. Coached her up
To keep the focus sharp on the country's needs.
Said, Always watch your flag. If it goes limp
Stiffen it with the starch of rhetoric.

She was eloquent. And had the proper voice.
She had the words. She also had the poise.
And when she ended with a couplet from Tagore
They clapped and said, You have put things rather well.

The others too had their say, following her.
Some whispered soft. Some raised their voices high
Some banged the table. Some passed their scripts along.
A turbaned woman from Somalia
Cried out loud (she could be heard a mile)
How awful that some people starve and die
While others have a ball and live in style!

The white men winced. Outlined their strategies
To change it all. Restore the grammar to the global scene.
Dot its *i*'s to follow cross its *t*'s.
Which meant, go green the earth and plant more trees.

The rich had the money; so had the final word.
There will be want for a few more centuries,
They sagely said. And with authority.
In the coming one, one quarter can be fed.
And at that rate,
We shall have to wait,
Three more to reach the goal.

But what about the rest? They can't last that long?
Someone intervened.
You are right, they said; but they never did.
And if they managed to
That will upset our laboured statistics.

There was a grand reception in the night.
She went there dressed in the colours of her flag.
And had to tell them what the colours meant.
They were more curious. That broad red spot
Upon your forehead, is that of menstrual blood
Or something else to seem? They said they got
That bit from a special feature in *Le Monde*.

She smiled and said, It is a public sign
To advertise the power of our sex.

That alarmed them. Again the gender talk?
For those who declared, *Vive la difference*,
This was distasteful. So they took the chance
To pay her a compliment. Your dress is fabulous;
And on your body it does show off best.
While, here, our girls resemble rolled cigars
When they wrap them on, having nothing on their chest.

But they have other things, she consoled them
They have those eyes sparkling from blue to brown;
Masses of wavy hair; those varnished lips,
That rhythmic bounce in the movement of their hips
That knocks our men down flat. And some of you.

That flattered them. But they won't leave her yet.
Do you have sex outside your married life?
She paused a while; then said with emphasis,
In the years before, but never afterwards.
For after that you have a full-time pet
You can call upon to perform when you like.

That would be boring, surely! They observed.

Ah, boring, yes. But that the whole thing is,
Whichever body you may take to bed.
The pitching up and down, the mealy spills.
The messed-up sheets, the scramble for the loo.
Though each may have his kind of body smell.

She is smart they said, a dyed-in-the-wool Hindoo
Who knows her *Kamasutra* through and through.

When the party was over they all bid farewell.
Some hugged, some kissed each other, some shook hands.
And one by one they went back to their lands
By the next day's morning flight.

In the aircraft's cushioned seat,
She was half-asleep
When the hostess came and announced the morning
    snack.
She waved it off.
Thought of the hectic day
That was her yesterday.
The little scenes of the funny shadow play
In which she played a role, a silly role.

But it was fading out;
She was looking forward now to getting back.
To Sadiq—Oh, my Sadiq! Where are you?
Instead of going to plead at the global bar
Why can't we both do something where we are?

FARM BIRDS AND FACES

Between two clumps of reeds
Bhumi and Bhudhan meet.

She is brown like the ploughed-up earth.
He is black like the monsoon clouds.
But their eyes are pink and silver.
Like two pairs of sun-baked moons
In which they see festooned
A message that warms their hearts
And makes their blood run wild
And crow like a crowd of cocks
Unscrewed by morning light.

The day grows white and warm.
Unlocks the bottled winds
From the padlocked racks of trees.
The farm birds flee their coops
In wayward witless groups,
Flailing their necks about,
Or float down the buoyant air
That layers the breathless walls.

Then arching from eye to eye
They see their lives' skyline.
All kinds of visages
Happy, unhappy, sad.

Nailed into hollow frames,
Stacked close to each other.
Some crowded with bands of colour.
Some criss-crossed with wiry line.
Some cut into sharp profiles,
Some ground into shapeless smears.

Though they are still in their teens
They recall the countless scenes
They passed in their childhood years.
The peep-show of birth and death
Between four walls of mud
Beneath a palm-leaf roof.

Some gilt with the glow of mirth.
Some blue with a throttling grief
Coming as the warp and woof
Of the lives they had come into.

Like the seasons of this earth
That followed each other out.
Now a cascade of silken blooms
In the wake of a laughing spring
Or the death of twig and leaf
In the blast of the summer winds.
Moving from scene to scene
As in a patua's painted scroll
Ending in the final frame
Of the death-god and his crew.

All these pan into view
In the backdrop of their eyes
On one side a faceless ghost,
On the other a god-like child.

Will all this choke and kill
Their bodies' inner call?
There is no chance it will.
The sound of the low drum beat
That rolls in their heaving chests
And the bounce in their arms and feet
Will never let this be.

They will lead them to soon decide
For the rough and rocky ride.

She will run for the bamboo shoot.
He will go for the hibiscus.

THE ODALISQUE AND THE JUMPING CAT

She sits now in a chair
Upon a tiger pelt.
Is that real or fake?
That will be hard to tell.
It has the orange field.
It has the jet black stripes.
It has a whiskered face.
And two balls of shining eyes.
And rows of teeth and claws,
All white like chinaware.

It is late afternoon
And like all such afternoons
Weighed down by a sense of loss.
Time is now running out.
The white day has lost its gloss.
She is just half-awake
Untied her body's knots.
The flesh has now become dough.
The skin too is creasing up.
The bones creak at every move.
The breath has a distinct wheeze.

But she remembers—once
Time stopped and served her ends.

(Or so it seemed to her.)
Burnished her moony face,
Tinted her cheeks and lips,
Buoyed up her tiny breasts,
Padded her waist and hips
Hardened her marble thighs,
And although she stood on earth
Flew her up in the skies.

Then the tiger was not a pelt.
He stood on sturdy legs.
Burned bright and waved his tail.
And held warm between her thighs
Breathed fire like a blacksmith's forge.

This gave her immense power.
Grew on her many arms
With tools for love and war
To handle any man or beast
That chose to cross her path.
Giving her a god-like grace
That redressed her mortal frame,
Burnished it silver white
Like a blistering autumn cloud.

But the tiger soon lost its power,
To hold high her body's fire.
So on a summer's day
He packed up and ran away

And jumped into a weedy lake.
She sought him; but too late.
When out of its slimy bed
They lifted and brought him out
He was already stiff and dead.

So on these hapless afternoons
She has no power-cat.
Only its ragged pelt.
Nor any beasts in sight
To give her a chance to fight.
No challenge now, no risk
So sprawling in her chair
And dreaming of the days gone by
She is no goddess now
Just a handsome odalisque.

THE POOL

Stone-lined the shimmering pool.
Steps of laterite that run down deep
To the velvet of the waters.

For some a magic mirror

Where they can see their faces
In a tantalizing blur.
Pregnant with promises
Of newer incarnations
With recharged life and power.

Or a bath of cool sapphire
To quench their body's fire
(Without the sweat and stress
And the washed-out emptiness
Of the usual things they do.)
Within whose laughing cover
They stripped down to their skin
And discovered passages

To a world there is within
Where wishes bloomed like sea-flowers
And incandescent fish
Touched their tiny nerve cells

With a shock of thrill or pain
And rimmed their round horizons
With a ring of coral light.

One can still recall
Those days when you were small
There were pools in town and village.
Where crowds of people met
Boys, girls, the rich and poor,
The aged and the young.
Where through the livelong day
They heard the temple bells,
Drums, pipes and ritual chants
And the rumbling roll of prayers.
Where they sat and dreamt
Under the shadowed covers
Of the skirting corridors,
Of lives they longed to live
Not the ones they had chanced into.

Letting their wandering minds
Step down the water's edge
Into a land of green and gold,
Where reigned the serpent king
And his bunch of dazzling queens
Who held in their bejewelled heads
The secret spells for change

(Or so the story went)
And could teach them to unwind
And moult from role to role.
Change their dress and speech,
Alter their body rhythm,
Even hopes and horizons.
And become someone else.

That led the old to dream
That they could still run wild.
And the young to hate
Being treated like a child.
They liked to burst their seams
And leap out of their skins.

So the son of the land-owner
Sick of his pampered life
Desired to slog and sweat
Like a ploughman in the sun
Whistle and spit and swear
And slough off all decency.
Have legs like iron pipes,
And arms like husking pestles.
And lay those brawny girls
(Who make their wishes plain
With various body signs)
In the damp and shady furrows
Of the fields of sugarcane.

But the lowly peasant's son
Wishes to live in style.
Be served by rows of men
Who bowed and did his bidding.
And his lazy days beguiled,
In a many-chambered mansion
Hanging with velvet drapes.
Where his lean and elfish wife
In her muslin dressing gown
Would pet him like a child
And pat him down to sleep
(Without working him hard
Like his shameless Nelly did
Holding him in the vise
Of her tough metallic thighs),
Then herself dozed away
In careless disarray,
Lacing the moonlit air
With a mild decorous snore.

Then the girls who rued their fate
Of being the second sex
And wanted to do away
With their pads of waxen flesh,
Reline their level chests
With a coat of carapace.
Walk straight and wave their limbs
As their rough-neck brothers did,

Meeting them face to face,
Trading them blow for blow.
And feel in their underbelly
A stiffening machismo.

Or those dainty boys
Who sought to soften down
Their muscles and their skin
With depiling wax and cream,
Dust them with sugar and spice
And all that is labelled nice,
Paint their lips and nails,
Blacken their fluttering eyes,
Speak with a piping voice,
And with a wiggly gait
Sashay down the street.

Then those shining youth
And all those star-eyed girls
Who wanted to ferret out
The truth hidden in things
And use their secret codes
To fashion themselves wings
That flew them to unknown skies
Or changed the shape and size
Of the world that they inhabit,
Altered the reigning modes
Of the lives they had learned to lead.

Or carried them sliding down
To their mind's circuitous crypt
Where a sudden surge of light
Swept all their shadows out
Undid their inner knots
And ground down their silken tow
To an all-consuming glow,
Concluding everything.

Some made it. Some did not.
Some could not cut the knot,
And flee from their fated roles.
But the fat of their poolside dreams
Softened their inner cores
And loosened their attitudes.

Are these pools there still?
Do people sit and dream?

They are there hopefully.
As it is where they get a view
Of a piece of that submerged sky
That gives them a chance to see
Their given identity
As also turn it over
And read on its underside
Their still unfulfilled needs.

And in that light rescript
The roles that they inherit
Or unwittingly choose.
Thus put back the missing part;
Or make a fresh new start.

So the pool is, in one count
A hallowed baptismal font.
But seen in another light
It is the fervent site
Of a possible resurrection.
One auguring rebirth,
The other quickening the dead.

THE VISITOR

He does not knock, he is inside already,
He comes through walls and doors, steps forth from the pleated drapes,
Drops from the vaulted ceiling.
The Visitor.

He comes with many masks, and speaks in many voices.
He is both young and old; sometimes shy, sometimes bold.
He floats through the murky shadows, or rides on a shaft of light.
The Visitor.

When you lie down to rest, he falls into your sleeping bed
In diverse forms and guises.
The Visitor.
Imp, fairy, goblin, nymph
Or gorgeous demi-god
Who tricks or teases you, or warms your limbs and heart
And rouses into action that limp, lethargic snake,
Lying cold and coiled in your backbone's basal knot.
The Visitor.

But he is not always *he*
Or *she*. He can be *it*.
Things of various shapes and body or diverse names and forms
Sometimes just an airy feeling,

An electric vacancy.
A hooded mist studded with probing eyes
That hovers over your head and scans your sleep.
A flying apparition, bird, angel, moth
That comes to bless, or warn, or summon up
The sleeping daemon in your frozen blood.
A soundless thrill that crawls between your legs.
An unsettling dream that sets your mind astir.
A glow of light that paves your floor with gold
And tips all things around with a glittering edge.
A whispering voice that dogs your loneliness
Keeps you in conversation. Asks you the how and why
Of everything you do or do not do;
Cracks jokes, tickles your ribs and makes you laugh.
Peps up your mood and banishes your blues;
And paints your barren walls with rainbow hues.

A shade of absence that walks the world with you,
Leads you to strange locations. Barren fields,
Or woodlands thick with trees, under skies of searing light
Or sodden grey, mottled with many colours.
With fan-shaped palms, hand-shaped clumps of grass,
Eye-shaped flowers. Or swollen heart-shaped fruit.
Not what you are used to but genuine all the same.

Perhaps more genuine than the bland reality
Of day to day. For with their falsity
They strike an unknown chord within your core.

This upsets your measured plans.

And flashes messages. White script on glowing green.
The beaten path can't lead you very far.
The programmed search can't take you all the way.
The chosen word is too dumb to have full say.
You have to jaywalk, transgress boundaries,
Jump over fences and grope in the puzzling fog
For the magic root that will charm your fumbling steps
And bring you to what you seek.

They leave their marks,
These abrupt Visitors.
He, She or It,
In their elusive ways.
They never let you rest, they hound your days;
Or like clouds of moths they settle on your nights.
Keeping your mind awake the whole time through.
Pumping with life a weak and struggling breath.
Seeding with dreams a sleep sinking to death.

ODD ENCOUNTER

He stands in the shadow on one side of the road
She is framed in a spot of light on the opposite.

His eyes are red and rheumy, his mouth a shapeless fold.
Her eyes are varnished with all the hues of hope.

He whistles along the pavement; his eyes seek hers;
Her smile is the moon's first quarter; she does seem to care.

But they stay across the road, sticking to where they are
The distance is what ties them, nearness may keep them far.

He wonders what will happen if he steps out into light.
She also starts to think why can't I move across?

But they do not venture. The road is badly split
Into strips of sun and shadow, almost like day and night.

Some day in the time to come, when the light covers both sides
Or the deepening shadows will sink all difference,
The crossing may be easy. And they may make the choice.

THE MIRROR

See that face in the mirror
Half of it is beast.
Barbed and ravenous, eyes red-veined with rage.
White fangs of hunger. Black horns of hate.
Mouth warped with rank unreason.

It looks on everything
As an object of desire,
To be chased and overpowered,
Struck down and preyed upon.

But the other half is angel,
Shining and silver-soft,
Made up of as it were
Moonbeam and morning air.
Whom no sin can sully
Or shadow overspread.

For it goes to woo
The thing it wants to win.
Trying its best to please,
Not bring it to its knees.

But they are there together,
Both, tailored edge to edge.
So the angel is not all angel,
Or the beast a complete beast.

THE CIRCLE

A plant in a pot.
Twisting from root to leaf.
At one end the cloven sprouts
Edged with emerald. At another
The buds that hold the promise
Of future growth.

The shrinking stem below
Shakes off the drooping leaves.
Their ribs have lost the grip.
Their green has been reduced
To a muddy grey or brown.

One side a restless urge
To fly up and touch the sky.
The other a pressing wish
To stoop down and kiss the earth.
Between the skyward sprouts
And the leaves that fall to earth
Revolves the endless tale
Of birth and life and death.

Tara had twins.
They hang on her tiny breasts
Or grope around her waist

Tickling her skinny midriff.
But she does not mind.
When they chew her swollen tits
She does not feel the pain.
Instead,
A wave of pleasure wells up in her chest.
And her eyes go white with breathless ecstasy.

They drank her blood and shared her scanty breath,
Then ripped her body open to come to be.
She groaned and writhed. But all that blood and pain
Seemed worthwhile when she saw them in the crib.
You sweat, you spit, shed tears, you puke and pee
But to bring forth new life is a miracle,
Even if it takes you near the gates of death.

They are son and daughter. So much alike and yet
So different. Eyes like diaphanous clams
With a black pearl set in each.
Cheeks like downy peach.
Hands like moulded silk
When they close or open. Faces
Lit by smiles that mix moonbeam and milk.

Tridib is mostly out. But when he is home
He spends all the time with them. They are his world.
The house resounds with cheer. He sings and shouts,
Clowns around and dances. Says serious things
In the silliest words that float around like feathers

And settle on some spot near your heart.
When Tara mentions the problems of day to day,
Her fears and anxieties and forebodings,
He wraps them in his laugh and throws them out.
Says, Take it easy, dear. The wheel of time
Will cut the knots and solve your problems, all.
It has its logic. So, take life as it comes.
Let us live our lives as well as we can do.
Fill them with hope and cheer. Not kill them with fear.

He knows at heart that the logic he talks about
Is a heartless one. It honours nobody.
It lets one moment wipe out another;
Rolls good and bad in mindless succession.
Night gives way to day, the day to lightless night.
One unseats the other. Seasons come and go.
Rains come with tornadoes, the spring with flu,
The summer, German measles. But the monsoon clouds
Lace-bound with lightning are just fabulous;
The flowers of spring sow madness in your limbs,
And the summer sun burns craters in your heart
Releasing dreams you thought were dead and lost.

This logic of things adds up to a neutral grey
When you take them together—add greens to reds
Mix blacks with brilliant yellows. The only way
To save your life is to weave a rainbow web
With your little acts against its barren void.
Splash it with colour. Flood it with sound and song.

Tridib, cries, Tara, we are no longer young
But we have to be to see these on their feet.
She meant the twins he held in his calloused arms.
Surely, that long, he says. Then let them free
Like birds their young when they can use their wings.

Longer, says Tara, this is a dangerous world
Where men are beastlier than beasts themselves.

Smiling his smile, Tridib then asks, How long?
As long as Darby and Joan? Then catching her
He takes her to the window and says, Look down
And see them in the park beside their house.
Sitting on a painted bench in the mid-day sun.
His twisted hands holding her twiggy ones.

Darby had had a stroke last January;
Was in the nursing home for thirteen weeks.
His handsome face has lost its symmetry.
His hands and feet don't do what they are told.
He sees, now, haloes wherever he looks.
The angels are here to plan my final ride,
He mumbles, smiling. But Joan is nearly deaf.
She does not hear his words. Just gives a nod.
The erstwhile beauty queen is small and wizened.
Quilted with wrinkles. The polyps in her nose
Don't let her freely breathe. The pains in her bones
Don't let her turn around.

Tara, says Tridib, if we live that long
We shall be useless to our little things,
For all the love and care within our hearts.
Only a burden, to mar their sunny days.
How can we help them when we can't help ourselves?
So, when they are fit to do things on their own
We should withdraw. And take our final bow
When our legs are strong and our minds are quick and clear.

Tridib kept his word. One evening
He came home in a rattling ambulance.
His friends said he was in great spirits all day
But it couldn't last beyond the afternoon.
They put him on the bed. He seemed to sleep.
But his face was greyish blue and lips chalk white.

Tara broke down and fell a shapeless bag
Of flesh and bones across the hapless bed.
The air froze in the room that was till then warm.
The sinking lights showed the play was over now.
The one who walked will no more lift his limb,
The one who talked will no more move his tongue.
His blood will clot. His flesh will slowly rot
To feed the maggots. Unless they burnt it up.

A white bird flew with a blue moth in its beak
Leaving a cloudy trail behind its tail.

Tara revived. She knew this was to be.
He who lived day to day knew how to die.
She had looked beyond. So the fringes of her life
Got caught on the hooks and nails lined on the wall.

But, worn to shreds, she too will cease to be.
Some day. Wishing that it was earlier.
Leaving the twins behind to live their lives.

THE ANNUNCIATION

The angel dived to earth like a falling star
And whispered low, Please do not panic, dear;
The loop of fire that burns within your heart
Will step out as your son. And fatherless.
Without a home or roof. On a pitch-black night.
In the light of a blazing comet. Amidst a host
Of calving cows. And stacks of new-mown hay.
But when the world will see him at the break of day
They will call him son of man or son of god.
Though he is your son, your own, your sole device
To save a sorry world.
Then she touched her chest to toughen her tender soul.

It happened as she said.

On a pitch-dark night sailed in an eel-shaped star
Lashing awake the sky with its burning tail.
Her body arched in pain and split in two.
And from between her legs came out the child
Black-skinned and bright. He was too big to cry.
His downy face was floodlit with a smile.
His shiny back was blood-marked with a cross.

She read the message. She knew it from the start.
He was hers; but, yet, he would belong to all.

Born fatherless, he had home in every house.
He would save the world but would not save himself
As he had to give his lessons through his acts,
His suffering. And bid them do the same.

For, this world is built of fighting opposites.
Black and white. Yellow and violet.
When you hold to one the other is close behind.
When you do one good it hurts another one.
When you save a pigeon you starve a hungry hawk.
When you cage the owls the rodents rule the earth.
This makes you wonder, what is right? What wrong?
Crazes your head. And callouses your heart.
So you feed your needs and slowly turn to beast
Living for yourself or your pack or herd.
This has been so from the time of Abel and Cain.

But man has things within his inner core
That can salvage him. Alter his horizons.
Weave harmonies out of the warring strands.
The secret lies in seeing one's own face
In those of other men, even beasts and plants.
And deal with them like we wanted to be dealt.
This needs no law. Only a change of mind.
And courage to act. If needed bear the cross.

She had worked this out even when she was small,
When her neighbours fought and tore each other down.
But girls were barred from speaking on such things.

Only cook and serve. Dress up and please the boys.
She swore within that she won't let this be.
If she can't speak she would bear a son who would;
All on her own, untouched by mindless men.

And as the angel said he came to be.

And when he grew, he sat upon a mount
To forge a link between the earth and sky.
To get the body break the bonds of flesh,
To free the mind from its inbuilt manacles.
His home-spun words smelt of the dusty earth,
The pathless winds and pollen of the skies.
He spoke to herdsmen, he spoke to fishermen,
He spoke to tradesman and the wily rich.
He kept them captive with his simple speech.
His earnestness. And lack of rhetoric.

If you see your face in faces of other men
You will learn to love them as you love yourself.
Feel their joys and share their aches and pains,
This will break the walls that divide you each from each.
And weld you into a seamless family.
To hold in common the bounties of the earth.
Not scramble for a portion for yourself
And spend your days trying to keep it safe.
This will turn the water of your wanton lives
To the deathless wine of warm fraternity.
Your scanty bread will reach all hungry mouths.

Your meagre fish flavour all eager tongues.
You may have little but will be happy still
And feel like kings within your humble yards.

Some heard this eagerly; some laughed it out.
He thinks each face is like a looking glass!
They sniggered. While the others went to think
He was a kind of devil's advocate
Who sought to cheat them of their hearth and home.
So there he was amidst the crowded streets
Encircled by a friendless wilderness.

The talk of kings worried the enthroned kings
And their entourage of slaves and hangers-on.
They saw his words appealed to many hearts
And feared they may upset their apple cart.

Too dumb to read the meaning of his words
They had him caught. And nailed upon a cross.

The earth-mother stood and wept. In the steel grey clouds
The sky-mother sat and slept with swollen eyes.

PURVAPALLI SONNETS

1

This Purvapalli is a special place.
Its roads are gravelled with old memories,
Its bushes sigh, its hedges put out sprays
Of telltale flowers. Its enormous trees
Bear marks of ancient loves. They all remind
Its aged residents of their vanished years
Which with pick and broom they laboriously mine
For frozen rings of laughter, fossiled tears.
They show you these and chant their history.
And of the bard who set up this *house of peace*
Sang moving songs; taught them what to be,
Refined their minds and remade them piece by piece.
All varnished tales with bright plumage and wing
Where pleasures rise to top, pains lose their sting.

2

The day we came it was raining all the way.
The windows of the train didn't show much through
Of the land they raved about. The bright red clay,
The undulating earth, where the wild winds blew
The ground smells into air; where the laughing trees
Waved their heads and danced. When we got down
It was still wet and grey. A row of geese
Hobbled and quacked in line. When we left town
In open rickshaws our hostess smiled and showed
The trees that lined the road, loaded with white,
Lilac or yellow flowers. Then came the board
Marked *Golden Boat*. This was our camping site.
Just a painted boat? Or a half-moon sailing high
In the star-bloom crowded waters of the sky?

3

Three spacy rooms. An open veranda,
Facing the eastern sky. Where you could sit
And watch the world around and slowly draw
Your inner phantoms out from the dimly lit
Tunnels of mind. And ramble in-between
Sounds with shapes, amorphous images,
Lost things, remembered things, fragmented scenes;
Events and objects scrawled on the musty pages
Of age-worn memory. The strange quietude
That this place wove with sounds of many kinds,
The cricket's chirp, the cries of distant birds,
The cattle in the field, slowly unwinds
The rolled-up scrolls. Surely a perfect site
To recharge these and lift them into flight.

4

On the northern side a squat pomelo tree
Towards the south a broad and tall *simul*
And in-between a blank sky hanging free
Rippling with light, now warm, now dark and cool.
Rose red at dawn, changing to glowing grey
As the hours pass. At noon time silver white;
Blue in the afternoon. But at the close of day
A figured quilt. Then amidst the shades of night
Black gauze or satin threaded with liquid gold;
The backdrop for an engrossing passion play
You put together and act by act unroll,
Of things you sought to have, or having threw away.
Caught in this game you forget your daily chores
Even the bubbling ferment of your inner core.

5

An inner core? Is there an outer one?
Surely there is; made of our open thoughts
That hide the sources from where they are spun—
The fervid urges, the indefinite clots
Of unformed ideas we grapple with.
A seething underworld with passages of light
And pools of darkness mixing facts and myth.
When we paint and innovate or speak or write
We seek to hit this site whose miasmic air
Motivates our search and redefines
Our ends and means; alters the total fare,
Both the basic substance and accessory signs.
So every time we face the open sky
Our minds outline a novel route to fly.

6

But all the same this dark intriguing space
Is full of frustrations. Its pressing call
Inflames your heart and sets your head ablaze
With restless longing but puts a stolid wall
At the very gate you seek to enter through;
Befogs your paths, implants your route with snares
And when you manage these, leaves you no clue
Of the destination; which too disappears
The time you come to it, unless you grip its arms
Wrestle it down and pin it to the earth.
So, driven though you are by its doubtless charms
You come sometimes to doubt the real worth
Of all this effort and the derring-do;
A doubt, alas, you cannot hold on to.

7

A wave of joy runs through the waking earth.
The sunlight sings. Within the wind-blown trees
And flowering shrubs there is explosive mirth.
White butterflies float in the swirling breeze
Like airborne smiles. Bird calls fill the air
Do they call you by name? At least you feel they do.
Come, join our choir. And climb the sky's steep stair
And beat up a celebration the whole world through.
But a sudden wail cuts through the festive air.
Someone in pain? A suffering beast or child?
This tears down the tapestry. Holes it with fear.
Muddies the mind; makes your thoughts run wild.
The way things are we are born to live between
The good and the bad in this oddly mixed-up scene.

8

So the world seems at one time a carnival
Gay and colourful. Cross-hatched with light.
At another time it is as dour as hell.
Where everything is dyed in the hues of night.
In each one's life these visions alternate.
This is Nature's law. So it's best to fix one's eyes
On the brighter side of things. Patiently wait
For the clouds to clear. Then cruise the open skies.
Didn't someone say the mind is its own place
Can make a heaven of hell, a hell of heaven?
That a change in focus can bring the reds and greys
Or white and blacks to peace within its den?
So take things as they come, the wise men say.
The wheel will turn; nothing is there to stay.

9

Our pleasures are anchored in our body sites
The head, the heart and the diverse other spots.
No Eden stocked with all the canned delights
Can lead to these unless they hit the slots
Which they rarely do in ease and idleness.
You need to fight to win your paradise;
Enter the fray, go through storm and stress.
To be fully there you have to pay the price.
A pain-wrecked body savours a pleasure more,
A hungry mind moves straight to the core of bliss.
That pain and pleasure are part of the self-same score
They come to see. Neither can they miss.
Things are like that. When you arrange the bits
You see you can't avoid the opposites.

10

Raucous clouds and rude rapacious winds.
Blinding cracks of lightning. Swirling trees.
They unhinge your doors. Rip apart your blinds.
Set your senses humming like a swarm of bees
Crazed by the wildness of a wilful queen.
Old faces float upon your mind's mute walls.
Brown-haired Nan whose eyes were deep sea-green.
Doe-eyed Dahlia, fair-skinned but false,
Rahim who stuck to you like a flesh-locked twin
Till death took him; age-harrowed mum
Who stood by you, saw you through thick and thin.
Frame by frame. But foggy as they come.
On normal days they all keep stacked away.
To download them you need a stormy day.

11

All random clippings from old memory.
Visuals clear, but stories imprecise;
Or vice versa. Where shades of worry
Scramble with sparks of hope, truth with lies;
Making secret fodder for the lives we live
When a change of weather releases them to us.
Old faces mould the new. Old events give
A novel dimension to what the present does.
When the storm settles, a strange glow fills the sky
And sets you floating in a timeless space
Where all things mix; there are no cut and dry
Markings of what once was or is in place.
When you watch the calendar, the date pads grin
The months and years blur; the numbers spin.

12

Age tones down certain things; keys up the others.
Befogs the near, brightens the distant past
Those sharp-eyed birds bedecked with brilliant feathers
Are what you have not seen for ages last.
But they cry and cross your mind quite often now.
You saw them last when Sue was in your arms
Fifty years ago in a mango grove.
A lucky sign she thought. Then the row of palms
That fenced the horizon; which she called sentinels
Of that ageless moment; now few and far between.
Their image still survives and rings the bells
That bring to view a long-forgotten scene.
So some remembered things are fossil-clear
While the things around fade off and disappear.

13

A drenching shower. Then a spell of steamy heat
That caps the kamini with a froth of flowers.
Their fragrance maddens you. Quickens the bear
Of your sluggish heart. Rouses your sleeping powers.
In the looking glass your eyes are framed with grey
Your mouth is puckered with a nameless pain
The face is sallow, the skin furrowed like clay,
Pitted with scars; mottled with warts and stains.
But someone asks you, lifting the teapot's lid
You were handsome once; did girls get after you?
You can't remember. And even if they did
You were too engrossed with other things to do.
Now age has run its cartwheel on your face
You have had your day. You are no more in the race.

14

It was not fully true. When you were small
Two pig-tailed cousins showed you the difference
Between their body and yours. Then near the garden wall
Sri taught you how to kiss. Jay made you cross the fence,
Run to the seashore and roll between the rocks,
Hear the sea waves roar below your heart.
Her eyes were garden-green. Her brown-black locks
Smelt of salt and thyme. We had to part
When they packed up and sailed to Singapore.
I moped some days. But then came Josephine
Whose body smells seeped into your inner core
And drove you mad. And this revived the scene.
Older, she showed you all there was to do.
But that was years before I chanced on Sue.

15

The body's surge doesn't take much time to sag
The breathless thrill punctures and leaks awa
They are shortlived. The acts lowers their flags;
The smells turn sour; flesh loosens into clay,
The ground turns grey and the sky grows lustreless
And every time you repeat this exercise
It is the same old story, more or less.
But then came Hema with wide open eyes.
Into the neighbourhood. She had everything
About her that could turn your head.
The looks, the speech, the laugh, a surprising
Aloofness in the eyes that almost said
Go easy boy; these are just the outer lace;
The real me is in the inner space.

16

And so it was; as all her attributes.
Were wrapped in a light that kept her clean away
From the body's reach. Even its hungry roots
Fed on its outer glow. One could even say
Her presence was icon-like. It drew you in
To a little sacred space behind its face.
Her conversation sent you in a spin
To ideas you were chasing all these days;
And made you see the world in a fresh new way;
Not like a grounded bug but an airborne bird.
Hema didn't last. She died in May,
Quite suddenly, without a parting word.
But she had altered me; refixed my sights.
Beyond the body ridge. Redrawn my flights.

17

Why do certain things move you to tears?
A piece of sky, a tree, the golden lights
Of a sinking afternoon? Or some sounds Pierce
The frozen stillness of your inner sites
And inflame their air? Or certain smells
Manage to sow a madness in your mind?
Something in them that moves and rings the bells?
Something in you that makes your flesh unbind?
Perhaps both; because they aren't fully they
Till they have called you out and talked to you;
And you too found within this interplay
A you outside the normal who is who.
The bard had spelt this out quite long ago;
Saying this is how our inner tissues grow.

18

We are part of Nature; still we are apart.
Though subject to its laws, something in us
Makes us defy them and learn the art
Of using them for our own purposes.
But we love a lot of things outside of these,
The rain-soaked woods, the shining sun-washed skies
The rippling waters, bird-infested trees
Anything that is, or walks or crawls or flies.
Each is a wonder if we have eyes to see.
And each infiltrates and builds a silent fire,
Under our ribs; unties and sets us free
To chase a nameless object of desire
That in our fables we call the *golden deer*
A phantom that drives you from here to distant there.

RENU-DI

See Renu-di. Long hair and laundered face.
Clothes stiff with starch. Eyes sharp like laser beams
That bounce off things and inventory a place.
The floor-mat, chairs; the novel colour schemes
Of the prints on the wall; the photographs of kin.
Talks of old times, when a tall and handsome Swede
Fell for her hair and copper-coloured skin;
And wanted to touch her breasts and see her nude.
Her hands-off look stopped him. But they are friends.
He's sent her a snapshot of his wife and son
Even this year with a scribble at the end—
You remember once your cold looks made me run?
She does. She stores that like an autograph.
I made him run, she mumbles with a laugh.

A slightly soiled laugh. All through these years
None sought to touch her breast or see her nude.
Her skin has lost its sheen. Now no one cares
To notice her hair. Her closed-door attitude
Drove of all suitors despite her diverse charms.
Now dreams invade her isle of loneliness.
Shadowy phantoms take in their arms,
Grope round her waist, rumple her dress.
Her muscles loosen under their unseen hands.

A white mist floats between her legs' divide;
Heart beats like drums. She fails to understand
This sudden breach in her solid wall of pride.
Why didn't she let this body have its fling
At the right time? Her life's first golden spring?

But when awake she is still the stubborn prude.
Whose head her playful nieces set on fire
With their skimpy suits whose seams they leave unsewed
And their noisy antics. She shouts and calls them near
And reels out a list of things they should not do.
The girls are delighted. They kiss her on her cheeks
Saying: Renu-masi, you don't have a clue
That in such dress you will look so smart and sleek
That the palli's papas will beeline for your gate.

She looks outraged. Thinks these girls are another kind.
They know their minds, don't stand around and wait;
Ungagged by culture, they have no crippling binds.
Her looks are stern but she smiles within her heart.
She is glad these girls have made a glorious start.

DEMAI-DA

Demai's true Hindu name is Dayamoy,
Meaning kind-hearted, which he couldn't live up to
For a bug in his brain forced him to fix his eye
On the oddities of what others say or do;
And hold them to ridicule, often unkind.
The limper's limp, the lisper's slip of tongue
The sad confusions of the deaf and blind;
Each one's frailty picked neat and strung
With juicy anecdotes. They did amuse
A witless audience for a little while.
But he bored them soon enough by his overuse
Of age-old gags and a generous dose of bile.
Somewhere in him they saw a gaping hole
That he found hard to fill and ease his soul.

So this restless proclivity to ridicule
The slips and mistakes of the men around;
Their accent, spelling, ignorance of rule.
Their dated ideas, their unsure grounds.
And standing high on his sightly swollen fee
He expounds how things are in the large world;
In London or New York his normal beat;
Their culture scene where you could see unfurled
The endless colours of their appetites.

Unsettling, yes; but attractive all the same.
We are dyspeptic here; we starve our sites;
Our most explosive acts are bland and tame.
To give the world we have nothing in store
Except scrambled quotes from Gandhi and Tagore.

He is right of sorts. But like a lot of them,
The so-called eggheads, he runs soon out of gas.
Then he dwells upon his cough and the yellow phlegm
That clogs his nostrils. And explains how it was
Made worse by the doctor's pills. Then the haemorrhage
That has hung broad flags in front of both his eyes,
Red to start with, now slowly turning beige.
Then the whining mosquitoes and the nagging flies.
He wanted to go back quick. (Do so, they say,
And consult a specialist from Harley Street.)
But he won't miss the mela just two weeks away
And forgo the noise and fun of this annual meet.
So they sit and plan how not to pass his house
Or cross his path till the seventh day of Pous.

DINNER AT NIGHT

She had called him for dinner at her little flat.
Twenty by twenty, with a tiny kitchenette.
Panelled bath, a store, windows that showed
Beyond the hedge the bright and busy road.
Burnished floor. A Manipuri mat.
A dining table, two chairs, a sofa set
Of which one piece could alter into bed.
The off-white walls had a row of shaded lights
And a print or two of ancient temple sites.

She'd put a pot of flowers near the door;
Spread on the table a kalamkari print;
Placed orange napkins, plates of Gaya stone.
Bowls of bone china, silver forks and spoons.
A cassette player inside the side cupboard
Had Amjad Ali playing on sarod.

All this in honour of her special guest.
Though they had known each other for donkey's years
Of late they had noticed that their heart-bells ring
At the sight of each other. He was an artist now;
And she a designer. He was working for a show;
She designed things for a joint called 'Rainbow'.

Artists have eyes for every little thing
She went to think; and so did her best
To build an atmosphere quietly aesthetic.
Not too much arty, overtly smart and chic.
Just a tidy space tuned up to register
The muffled texts of both their murmuring hearts.

She suggested early dinner; the last few nights
Lights blinked and went off every now and then.
They could eat by candlelight but those fluffy moths
And the black stink bugs would air drop on the plates
So come by seven, she said; or maybe earlier.
The fare would be simple; her cooking skills were small.
Fried rice and aloo dum. Chutney and curds.
For dessert, gingerbread flavoured with cinnamon.
Which she had learnt from Bani-di to bake.
For drinks, fruit juice. Nothing to blow his fuse.
She knew he was a strict vegetarian
And disliked alcohol of every kind.

He came at eight with a gorgeous bunch of flowers
And a string of reasons why he couldn't come on time.
She put her hand upon his mouth and said,
Relax, you are on time whenever you come.
He felt relieved and ate her with his eyes,
Her face, her neck, her slender collarbones
Descending step by step. Good gracious me!
Where was this nymphet hiding all these years?

He was overcome. He missed the handsome prints,
The table, flowers; the music and the mat.
And she didn't mind the least. They were just there
To clear the air and turn the spots on her.

They were both hungry. And both cried, shall we eat?
And they did too, sitting opposite each other.
He praised the food; she herself was amazed
That each thing tasted good. And the lights shone bright.
But when they had just finished the gingerbread
The lights went out. In a darkness black as jet
She steered him safely to the yielding sofa set.

What will they do for another hour or two?
Words drown in darkness; the famished eyes withdraw.
The only sense that works is the sense of touch.
So they held hands. Edged close to each other;
And before they knew were in one another's arms,
Since this was not easy in the place they sat
By slow degrees they slipped down on the mat.

This new location contrived a change of scene;
Transforming them to a state they had never been.
Two night-smudged faces; four hungry eyes
Glowing like ash-rimmed coals.
Steamy breaths that smelt of cinnamon;
Slavering mouths of saffron-scented rice.
Muffled cries that unwound one by one
Their two identities.

Reduced their bodies to throbbing lumps of meat.
Parts soft like dough; parts hard like a bouncy fish
In muddy waters. Amorphous, featureless.

Only the hands and feet
Kept shape and lashed around
Fired by a burning wish
To untie the knots; unsew the ridgy seams
And inaugurate the blind combat of flesh.

A fight to lose, or where to score a win
You had perforce to sink and surrender.

In this sightless night where was she, where was he?
They had loosened to fibre and lost their body shapes.
And their hard locations. They flew from earth to sky,
Strips of excitement, shivering like ticker tape.
He could feel his lips when her lips were pressed on them
She could sense her body when she was in his arms
Not otherwise. They needed each other.
A hot cloud smothers them. A hive of stars
Buzzed round and round humming an ageless tune.
Were they on earth, in water or flowing air?
Were they in one place or were they everywhere?

When the lights came on, they were there on the mat
Like sea-washed bodies rolled upon the shore
Of a strange new world. An island of their own.
This was marked on their skin and engraved in their bone.

When they got up to dress and looked at each other
They knew for sure they were not what they were
Some time ago. The message was everywhere.
To be fully each, they needed the other one.

VIVA KUNDERA

Milan is a fitting name for Kundera
For he brings to bed his various characters
As often as he can—on foot-worn floors,
Frayed carpets, creaking cots. In shaggy rooms,
Reeking of smoke and sweat and stale perfume.

Sex is to him a street of liberation
Inside a choking world. An arch of victory
For the hopeless waifs who are marked out for defeat
And limp from loss to loss; and on their lonely beat
Can't tell apart who is a friend or foe.
But wrapped in the blanket of their body heat
They are winners all on top or down below.

Pope Kundera peers down the mantelpiece
With probing eyes and sly demonic grin.

An unspelt sermon unrolls from his gaze.
Listen, boys and girls! Wipe out the sense of sin
Your minds are painted with. Fully erase
Those inhibitions that bind your hands and feet.

This inbuilt game is god-given gift to us
Where both sides win and none misses the bus.

Give up the roles you have been forced into.
For a little while. Undo your sashes, unclasp your belts
Discard your clothes and their sewed-on reservations.
The body is innocent when it is all itself;
Both the young and green and the hungry age-scarred ones.

A screw unscrews. Makes you forget the world;
Escape its traps and endless suffocations.
When you spiral up to its white orgasmic peak
In the yab-yum mudra you own the heaven and earth.

But when the spiral sinks and furls your flags?

You will have another chance to try again.
Life is like that. Nothing is there for good.
For all our longing for eternity
We can't see its face till it begins to flee;
A timeless spark that time soon whisks away.

THE PARTY

The sherry party before Michaelmas.
Professor C came round and filled the glass
The girls passed round the snacks.
There was some music; that did not drown the talk.

Small and well-dressed C walked around with ease
And talked to all. Though I can't now recall
What things they talked about
Culture, customs, art?
The news headlines?
The ubiquitous fog?

At first the sherry seemed quite innocent.
But with each succeeding sip it transformed them.
Opened new ventilators in their head.
Unlocked their words and made them freely flow.
Then made them mount each other or mixed them up.
Then mangled them into noisy gibberish.

Not all at once. But in slow degrees.

It worked wonders on the straitlaced Englishmen,
And the tightlipped girls.
Who were folded in and reticent by choice.
Ruptured their verbal hose and made it squirt

Wildly on every side. And speak of things
They never spoke to themselves in their beds.

Bald-headed Andrew spoke of his ancient gran
Of ninety years. She was still more agile
Than the youthful girls. And her deep blue eyes
Were much more ravishing than any of theirs.
Then the stories of her various escapades
That outshone Boccaccio's. I am part Italian,
She always claimed; not a sewed-up northerner.
No doubt, Andrew was deep in love with her.

Bill stood around in his elegant suit
Hands in the pockets, eyes in the air.
Peter, his brother, was in Russia presently
The. Queen's ambassador.
He may visit them at Christmas time this year.
And see the Hermitage.

Then he held out on
His various trips towards the east and west.
With spicy anecdotes to brighten them.

Then breezed in Patricia with a shock of thick brown hair
And caught me by the shoulder. How old are you?
Perplexed, I said, I am now thirty plus.
Are you kidding me? You don't look twenty yet.
But, by the way, what is Theosophy?
Or table turning?

The astral bodies they say we all have?
Have you read 'The Secret Doctrine' of Madame Blavatsky?
I could not help her much. I knew the names
But always bypassed esoteric lore.

George looked at me and winked from yards away.
He was frankly handsome. Was being preyed upon
By a hawk-nosed girl, who toyed with his blood-red tie.
You worked with Bill Reid and carved those totem poles
Straight on the sites in the Haida settlements?

Something she would like to do.
She had dreamt one night
That she stood in the open in her birthday pink
Getting painted black and red like those big poles.
Braving the winds against a blue-black sea.
Was that a sign? To show her origins?
Was a raven or beaver amongst her ancestors?

Kamal was trapped by Reg,
He lectured him.
About how to make it big on the sculpture scene.
Forget the surface,
Focus on cross sections.
Added, times have changed and with it the ruling tastes.
Lean girls with sallow butts and button breasts
Are more engaging now than the Rubenesque.
To pose for these he looked for Asiatics
Who still preserved their lovely famished looks.

Kamal was squirming; the girl he sought to meet
Stood just behind talking to someone else.

Now Angela. Who typed and kept accounts
Half-day at office. Then sold brushes and paints
In the shop below.
Or posed undressed before the drawing class.
She had a lovely torso, though her legs were fat.
She had done art but her reigning interest
Was in the art that was,
Of Egypt, Sumer, India,
Fabled mid-Asia and the distant East.
She will like to do art history if she can.
If they will make it lively. Not stuff it in
The musty tunnels of a mortuary.
For this she knew she'd have to struggle hard
For the next two years and save up all she can.
Her mum was in a home. Her brother a hopeless drunk.
So things would not be easy.
Then she quickly asked
Shall I bring you now another little glass?

Oh no, no, Angela; that will kill the fun.
Just as I am I can see the scene around
And hear what others say and enjoy it.
And talk to people sense when I have to.
A little more will badly mess things up.

It was already eleven.
The party was losing shape.

C had left. And Bill had followed him.
Voices were rising high. There were arguments,
Most of them silly; more full of sound than sense.
Like one between two boys who had come from Spain.
About who was better, Matisse or Picasso.
One called the former a carpet designer.
The other tagged the Spaniard a circus clown,
A contortionist and crude sex maniac
The room was choked with smoke; and the extra sherry
Had softened the tissues of their tiny heads.

George came and asked, shall we call it a day?
The last train to Barnet is half an hour away.
I nodded yes. And wished everyone goodnight
Then Patricia flew in with her flaming eyes,
Kissed George on the cheek and kissed me on the mouth.
See you again, dears, see you again; goodnight!

That was a torture.
The reek of a mouldy cheese
And unwashed teeth and garlic made me sick.
J ran in panic into the cold night air
Wiping my mouth with fury.
George laughed and laughed.
Don't rub off your skin, you will feel better when
You reach your room and gargle with cologne.

We caught the train and had a place to sit
Saw our diffused faces in the glass panes opposite.
Which made us smile.
If we overlay the images each one has
This is the laughing monster we shall end up as.

WHEN YOU CLOSE YOUR EYES

When you close your eyes and want to purge them clean
Of every speck of light and paint them black
It is not easy.
Phantom streaks of ghostly red and green
Tear across its back.
For the scripts you cook in the greenroom of your mind.
Trot out its figures in noisy fancy dress
On its empty stage
Even sleep does not bring peace; it is thick with dreams.
Spinning and dancing dreams with dragon masks
And bodies of ballet girls with lathe-turned limbs.

Even the colour of blindness changes from man to man,
The experts say.
It is black to Benode-da,
To Borges it is yellow.
To some others it may be violet.

Full blackness comes when you can kill your thoughts,
Say the grey wise men.
But why will you kill them, pray?
Did not someone say
You think therefore you are?

Why will you cease to be
To wipe clean a messed-up slate?

A LONG-LOST SUMMER

The hot wind burns like fever,
And sprays fine dust into the blinking eyes.
You feel you are dried up like a raw desert.
Broken clouds like little heaps of ash
Litter its forlorn sky
From near to far it seems a charnel yard.

On three sides of you the blazing terraces
On the roof above the flat stone-smelting sun.
The mind's maze of streets are deathly mute and bare;
Shadow-hemmed they shine like white-tinned brass.

But now and then a memory ambles through.
Of when such heat did not trouble your mind and body
But gave them a healthy shine like to mango leaves.
When you walked bare-head with Sue in the noonday sun
To the bank of the distant river
Where the sun-trimmed stream had shrunk to a measly ribbon
Plaited with deep tree shades.

RAIN-SOAKED EVENING

A rain-soaked evening.
Lights slip from the wayside poles
To the watery street.
Crawl on the damp sidewalks,
Sink into gaping cracks,
Laugh in the puddles,
Stick gems and pearls upon the wet tree leaves
Now lost to view.

The sky cloaked in mournful grey,
The houses in shapeless black.
From a window on the road-side west
Spills out a plaintive song
'Each time the koel calls
It impales my lonesome heart'
Everyone knows the words.
Also the haunting voice.
No doubt it's Begum Akhtar
At her soulful melodious best.

DOCTOR

This one, he said, is meant to soothe your nerves
This orange tablet to raise your appetite.
This striped capsule that seems a legless wasp
Has all the vitamins. That light pink pill
Will let you sleep right through the disturbed night.
If things get worse, I am there to help you out.

As reports go, things do not seem so good.
There is blood in spit. There is sugar in the blood.
There is pus in pee and worms and cysts in stools.
You are preyed upon by bugs of various kinds
Some sharply visible, some incognito.

This is Doctor Chatterjee, bright-eyed and bald.
Who comes to see me whenever he is called.
He keeps me informed of what is wrong with me.
In his able hands I feel quite safe and free.

But no medical man can buy you eternity.

Poems: Rhymes of Recall (2014)

RECALL

When my mum bore me she was far gone in years.
Had two grandchildren to feed and fuss about,
Who cried for their granny more than they sought
    their mum
And kicked up a row when she was not seen around.

So I learnt to share straight from my starting years,
The heart sank a little perhaps, but there were things
That buoyed it up and made it ride the waves.

The squirrel that learnt to eat from my tiny palms
And nibbled my fingertips with a laughing look;

The cat that rubbed its soft back on my legs
And miaowed to catch attention
With stiffening tail and wide imploring eyes;

The neighbour's daughter who took me on her lap
And tickled me with her chin
Her moist eyes glowing with kohl-lined glee;

The morning light that tiptoed into rooms
And danced on wall and floor
Amid the swirling shadows;

The kitchen sounds, the creak of the well-side pulley
The temple bells and drums and high-pitched pipes
That drilled a thrill through the hollow of my back.

These came unsought and kept me company.

True, my mum did come sometimes and hug me hard
Taking my breath away;
Watered my face with kisses and on some nights
Took me to bed with her;

We slept side by side under the silken cover
Of her body smells and of jasmine in her hair
Which sank deep roots in my nascent memory.

In my dreams these days I rarely see her face
But this haunting smell confirms that she is there.

THE FIRST ENCOUNTER

The bright and dew-drenched morning
Of a late December day;
After a busy night
When the ashram glowed with candles
Observing Christmas feast.

The mela has ended.
The tents and poles are down.
The ground is littered with hay and red clay cups
And bits of crumpled paper.

The crows cry hoarse,
Hop and pick around,
Squint with slanting heads.

The Santhal girls who danced the whole night through
Huddle and sleep under the banyan tree
Smelling of oil and sweat and mahua flowers.
Bleary-eyed, the young men sit in groups
Chat and giggle and pass the pipe around.

Going to collect my mail I chance on Lee
And with her a little girl
Wrapped in a ragged shawl
That concealed most of her

Except a pear-shaped head,
And flat, brown, floating hair.

Meet Sue, said Lee
She is a good old friend.
I greeted her
But she was too shy to smile
Just gave a silent nod.

The next few days I saw both Lee and Sue
All over the place.
The teashop, library,
The various studios.
The hallowed Havell Hall,
The sal-tree avenue.

She was being shown
The place she had seen before
About five years back.
In those few years
The place had changed a lot.

This showing unwrapped her.
In the next few months
When winter passed and spring time tiptoed in,
Costumed in various colours,
She burst her old cocoon
And stepped out with open wings.

Her pear-shaped head now seemed less like a pear.
Her soft profile had a moving tenderness.
Her eyes' white sparkle gleamed like a fishing bait.
There was a candid charm in her smiles and speech.

She was still withdrawn but knew how to draw one near
And hold one's gaze without any artifice.

What brought us close I don't remember now
But as time passed and seasons cycled round
This closeness spread and caught us in its web.

ON A RAINY DAY

It is hot and sultry. I am almost half asleep.
Lights dip and float blue shadows in the eye;
Ears hear a whine like that of a landing plane.

Then a sudden thud.
The airborne dream nosedives and hits the ground.
Jolted I see I am not in the air
But cooped up on the road in an auto-rick.

The crowds are running with hands above their heads
They fear a cloudburst soon.
The houses are mouldy. Large potholes line the road;
Dogs cringe and shiver in the mean and murky lanes.

A girl on the pavement mewls on her new mobile.
The boy in the shop bawls out the market rates.
Buy now, he shouts, tomorrow will be late.
Buy what, I wonder.

One time, the rains pumped up your head with dreams
Of nameless places you could go with Sue to see.
And you did too. Far from the normal haunts.

Their strangeness drew a halo round each site.
The hollow roads, the yellow hay-built huts,

The mud-brick ruins, the trees that grimaced wild.
The broomstick bush.

Tea in the wayside booth heavy with smoke and sugar.
The toothless smile of the grandma who mixed the brew;
That mooned above your head;
And asked you to come again.

Sue is not there.
My back has lost its spring.

And they have cleaned up the countryside;
Cut it with roads and ridges,
Felled trees, razed bushes down,
Ploughed the ground into a graph of measured fields,
Stuck boards of ownership.

The world is not open now
For you to walk across.
Between you and the far sky blue
There are numerous stiles and gates
You need to bargain through.

REACHING OUT

Strangely I wrote no verse
When Sue was still around
No rhyming epistles, no songs of love,
No romantic odes, effusive serenades.
We were sewn to each other
With various inspun threads
That left no place for words.
Mute looks were good enough
And their viewless magic web
That kept us intimate
Across dividing walls
And the spaces spread beyond.

And if some words there were
They came to fill the gaps
Or undo the sundry knots
In its delicate filaments
Or punch the secret keys
Of the mind-board set below.

To record the inner stories
Of the gropings, reaching out
The inborn thirst, the outward responses
The flow of fluid flesh

The giddy flights of senses
Their counter-wheeling dives
And the trails they left behind.

Now that she is not there
I try to dig these up
Straighten the tangled loops
Restore the time-worn links
Replay the faded score.

But the threads are gossamer thin
My efforts mess them up.

THE HEALTH WALK

The mornings are beautiful
The spreading sunlight wraps
Each little thing with gold;
Not just the leaves and flowers
Even the sticks and stones.

Birds sit on trees and sing
Flicking their tiny tails,
Or puffing their downy chests,
Or shaking a restless wing.

The doctor has tried to tell her,
He has done so many times,
Don't miss your morning walks
You need to work your lungs
And lose some needless weight.

She nodded in agreement
But smiled and said to herself,
That pompous baby-face!
For over sixty years
I have done this without fail
Wherever I have lived
Whether on the sun-baked plains

Or the cool Himalayan hills
Without needing such advice.

For she loved these daily sorties,
The sight of the smiling world
That stepped out of the night
The smell of morning breeze,
Sharp from the fresh-cut hedges,
Soft from the flowerbeds,
That quickened her flow of blood,
Kick-started her inner wheels,
Unlocked the body's urges,
Turned on its appetites.

But now she is another person,
The world is a different world.
The air has lost its lightness;
Runs slow and thick like mud.
Chokes her, abrades her nostrils
Makes her break into cough and sneeze
And when she tries to pick up speed
Drives her to pant and splutter.
Break into clammy sweat—

But daily an hour before daybreak
She starts out all the same
When calls from the mosques and temples
Coax people out to pray.

My walk is my prayer, she mutters;
Opens her gates and starts.

But before going fifty paces
'Happy,' her neighbour's dog,
Black-eyed, wet-nosed and hairy,
Jumps out and fawns on her
She pats him and tells him, Darling,
My hands are empty now,
Meet me another time.
Dogs are terribly civil
And quick to read the message
In whatever tongue it is.
He springs back to where he came from,
Leaves her to walk in peace.

Another fifty paces,
Between hedges of flowering henna
There under the jamun tree
Stands imperious Ruby-di
Her grey hair bobbed like a turban
A red cashmere round her neck.

Sue, stop for just a minute
In the shadow of this tree
I have so much to tell you.

It is always the same old story.
She had heard it many times,

Sometimes peppered with anger,
Sometimes soggy with tears,
With slightly altered details
Of the sorry life she leads.

Her husband's brittle temper
And his bleeding piles
That stains the shining covers
Of their bedspread every day
Which the prying mali laughs at
And the maid declines to wash.

Then their busy son's unconcern
About their little needs
And the covert machinations
Of his pretty dressed-up wife
Who she feels is training
Their monster of a son
To be their tormentor
Though he is hardly four.

He hides their books and papers,
Steals their writing tools,
Spills ink on their silken slippers,
Oil on the bathroom floor,
Plays with his grandpa's glasses
Instead of the teddy bear
That on his previous birthday
They spent a fortune to buy.

Then cries, Can you imagine
What he did yesterday!
He stamped those glasses to pieces
Under his shoe-shod feet
Seeing within their shadow
The shape of a scorpion.

To follow, his mother's lecture
On child psychology;
Mom, please don't brand him guilty
It will warp his tender mind
Your son will get new glasses
This time with golden frames.

Sue sighed and complimented
Her hairstyle and her shawl
To divert the conversation,
And put her in a better mood.
Then turned round and quickly called off
Her health walk for the day.

WEDNESDAY OUTING

Years have passed.
Each day now seems the same
Sunrise to sunset.

But once they glowed with colours
When Sue and I were young
And met in a landscape lined with little trees
Where a poet came to dream
Of training youth to man a brave new world
Where life will be a kind of sacrament
Connecting man and nature and man and man
And called the settlement
'The abode of peace'.

Where the toll of bells that woke you up at dawn
The bird-cries in the air
The smell of flowering trees
All, raised to roaring life
The silent spots within;

Where on weekend Wednesdays
People sat to pray
In a glass-built temple
And sang the poet's songs
That saw the face of God
In the heart of everything.

Where, when the prayers were over
And each one went his way
We skipped our breakfast and ran across the ridge
Over laughing pebbles and brittle crackling twigs,
Crossed the railway line
And came to a narrow gully lined with grass
Where we sat in secrecy
And talked the whole day through.

For a tongue-tied pair
This was a big surprise.
The smell of the earth, perhaps,
Unlocked the bashful shells,
And paved a passage through.

She came to Kashi when she was still a child.
Came motherless;
But the city made it up
Crowded with strangers at all times of the year;
All strangers saw each other as their kin.
So she found many mothers;
And scores of sisters too—
And a host of well-wishers and doting friends.

Then the river Ganga as broad as God's own chest
Whose waters took her in their limpid arms
When she entered it, as a loving mother would;
Caressed her body,
Kissed her anxious head.
And whispered things that soothed her sinking heart.

'Though it is rock and ice where I begin my life
I am worshipped here by a surging multitude;
But at the far end I fall into the sea,
A wild white sea that ends my existence.

Yet between the rocks and sea I laugh and live
Rubbing the ribs of earth, holding the sky
In the tiny mirrors of my glassy waves.
And in this passage I have many histories,
That grow and multiply with the passing years.'

The water's words infused her mind with dreams
Of various things to do.

On holidays she spent there many hours
And floated midstream like a living raft
Flat on the water, losing all sense of site.
Below the winkless gaze of a rimless sky
Making her feel she owned the universe.

She had many things to say of her previous days
Some pleasing incidents, some painful ones.
She went on and on
And while doing so
She also peeled me down to my inner core
With endless queries, unlacing my reserve.
Making me reel out the seaside episodes
Of my growing-up years.
And line them up like a row of mussel shells.

Between these ramblings we discovered each other
Found vacancies in each the other could fill
Noticed odd details we missed before
I saw a twinkle in her deep brown eyes
And an arc of mischief between her tiny lips.

She scanned my face and said You have two moles
On your left forehead which is a lucky sign.
I can trade you one of those, I laughed and said
If you can stick it where your eyebrows meet.

All silly talk to while away your time
Till you became sure you needed each other.

MISSED TRYST

The usual window I raise my eyes to scan
Is a vacant cage today.
Just a row of stubborn bars
Framing a blankness more opaque and dense
Than a solid stone-built wall.

The day is bright. Palms toss their leafy crowns
The road shines silver. Wind floods the laughing bush
The earth-banks splay their bare and shameless thighs
Along the grass-grown river.

Alone, I move to the green fields turning grey
Like a forlorn torch on fire.

I can saw the earth today with my body's edge,
Can clear the sky in a single long-legged leap
Plough down the river, half-water and half-sand.

But her absence darkens both the earth and sky,
Snuffs out all animation.
No sound of cattle bells, no peacock-cries
Just a choking silence among the jamun trees
That soaked with green our usual afternoons.

And voiceless water in the broken stream
Holding scattered fragments of a sallow sky.

SENSE OF TRUTH

Each person is
An endless continent.
For you to know another
You have to be
Stanley and Livingstone
Rolled into one.

Still you can't scale all peaks,
Or sail all streams,
And probe all recesses.
Like our skin covers
Our body's secrecies
Our words and thoughts
Hide more than they reveal.

And to think of it
Grave dangers lurk within
One's being transparent.

Nor can you say
There is one single truth.
All facts have foggy sides
And hidden implications.
And each of these
Has its own entrance gate
To a mixed-up middle core.

Besides to be with others
And live with them in peace
You can't say all you please.

See G.

There she comes waving her unsleeved arms.
Is dressed in a saree
That seems a coarse bed-spread
Patterned with ugly roses
Resembling bleeding sores.
And her awkward gait confirms
Her thighs are fat.

She stops and smiles.
And asks me how she looks;
Adding, I am on a diet
For one full hungry month.
(Surely on chocolate cream!)

I smile back and say
She looks just fabulous
(Without a clue what fable I refer to.)

But G is a nice girl,
Concerned, affectionate;
Does a lot of good to people
And offers help
When I am in a fix.

Why would I upset her
By saying how she looks
On this lonesome, luckless day?

Honestly, no one feels
Or looks the same each day.
On certain days
G is a tiresome bore
(Like I too tend to be).

Reels out endless tales
Of her faults and failures.
But on the following day
She is just glorious.
Has a gainful conversation
Beaded with sparkling wit,
Which weaves a golden halo
Round her radiant face.

Did not someone say
He experiments with truth?
Seeking to lay it bare, even evaginate!

If truth was one
And easy to lay hold on;
Fits like a clean round berry
In the pit of your tiny palm
Why would you need to go
For this arduous exercise?

But a lot of them insist
There is a basic truth.
That it is unchangeable;
And defies time and space.
They stamp their feet and say,
What is, surely, is.

But this is a matter
For semiologists to ponder—
What is, certainly, is.
But it carries all of us,
Sitting on its breast or belly
Or any other part of it.
We scan it with eager eyes
Like a housefly the apple tart.

And the tools we use for this
Whether the inbuilt ones,
Or those improvised
By hand, machine or mind,
The reigning moment and the mood
They all interfere.

So, for all its being there
We only see a part
Of the panoramic truth:
Which says more about the seer
Than the scene one seeks to see.

So this continuous search
For a way to put together
The numerous divided clues;
From the day we drop on earth,
Till the day we breathe our last.

THE RIDDLE

No man is happy with his happiness,
Not totally.
Inside its glow lies a shadow spot
That upsets him.
So behind his capers, whoops and beaming smiles
There is a nagging doubt,
Is this all true?

For his interests run on the self-same track
As those of many others.
And to get his place he has to deprive them,
To gather things he has to rob the earth,
Dig, pluck and pare, harvest or excavate.
Raise crops to reap, rear stock to kill,
Drain shining lakes, level the stately hills
And fill the sky with denigrating smoke.

And like all these things he employs to build himself
All those he learns to love and depend on
He brings to grief—
Parents, kindred, pals and paramours.
Even in love he is not fully sure
Whether he always functions as a wholesome mate
And makes his partner an equal accomplice
Or uses her as a passive implement.

This oddness is innate in Nature's laws
Which mark one creature as another's prey
Or nefarious aide; all fixed to serve
The other's end by instinct, not by choice.

A female mantis chews down her hapless mate
After he has seeded her.
A caterpillar nibbles the silken leaves
Of sprouting garden peas;
But most of them don't last quite long enough
To become butterflies:
As the banded wasps catch them and close them up
In arty cells of masticated earth
To feed their ungrown young.
Spiders catch flies with highly practised skills
But bulbuls eat both these with great relish
And float on open wings in the evening air.
Fish feast on fish but a big squid gobbles them,
The eater and the eaten in one enormous gulp.
To live, wildcats hunt down fleet gazelles
They outrun easily and overtake.

This dance of life, or death, goes on and on
And this is preordained.
So Nature is not as benign as it looks;
It has horns of discord below its waxen hair
And fangs of hate behind its smiling lips.

So most of us try to miss the shadow spots
And stack our eyes with those that remain bright,
Like an artist blinks to miss the odd details,
Of a complicated scene.

To be at peace we seek to rein our eyes
And keep them strictly on pleasure track,
See the blushing flowers and not the bugs within,
The full-grown fruit but not the concealed worm
And seal our ears with titillating sounds
To keep out the growls and barks and roars and squeals
And the cries of pain that upset our placid lives.

So the priests tell beads to keep their minds at rest.
The Krishna-buffs play drums and dance around
Singing the stories of their playful god.
Some take to drink to put their nerves to sleep
Or inhale drugs for a trip of ecstasy.
Some set themselves hurdles to overcome
Or fill their heads with dreams of various kinds.

But this doesn't change the world;
It is the same old scene
If you see it as Buddha did in his early days
From his hillside balcony
You notice that people age, fall ill and die
For all the noise they make about their lives.
And learn that happiness and a later sense of loss
Are siblings of a sort

That each leaf of pleasure is ribbed across with pain
For all its verdant sheen.

So the wise men say
True happiness is a sense of hueless peace
You come up to when you have reasoned out
These fights of interest
And face their passage with equanimity.

But this is philosophy
It may calm your mind but does not cool your heart
The heart is up in arms against this state
That offsets joy with pain, love with hate.
It yearns for a rainbow land whose cleansing rays
Will rid the world of its dichotomies
Plant in each creature a self-sustaining self
Each seed and stem and leaf and flower and fruit
Both eater and eaten like that mythical snake
Whose mouth swallows the body and comes to naught
Leaving behind a ring of radiance,
Which can unroll another round of life.

An empty hope? An insubstantial dream?

ART AND ARTIFICE

Under the bright tube lights
The grey walls are glowing white
But the floor is a sorry mess
With cups of dried-up colour,
And spills of unwiped paint,
Half-open rolls of paper,
Loose stacks of sketching pads,
Mugs holding brushes and pencils,
Trays heaped with colour tubes.

That is how it all should be
In an active artist's studio
Says Neera, walking in,
Flashing a knowing look.
Neera writes a weekly column
In a local newspaper
About art and eating places;
Explains with a naughty wink,
First food for the hungry stomach
Then food for the curious mind.

Then, turning a semicircle
Runs around her roving eye
Searching for a useful topic
For her next week's supplement.

And notices an open book
On the top of the working table
Titled *Art and Artifice*.
Settles down in a moda chair
Pushing her rather meagre butts
Into its yawning soap-dish seat.
Then lifting up her glassy eyes
Asks, What does it talk about?

I say, I haven't read it yet;
Presume it tries to tell apart
What comes to us with an inborn urge
And what we wilfully contrive.
Through most of the things we do
Fall somewhere between the two.

The first is like the artless art
Of the comely features of your face.
The other the diverse things you do
To make them much more explicit,
Like a dab of powder or dash of paint,
A practised look or gait or gesture
Or a cultivated smile.
This makes Neera self-aware,
Run a tongue on her shapely lips,
Smooth with hands her ruffled hair;
Then fixing her eyes on me
She asks, What does it say about the artist's art

Is that inherent in the artist's bone and flesh
Or attains its final shape
From practised skills and exercise?

This question makes you set your thoughts
On the subtle ties between the two
What comes to you at the time of birth
And what you choose to learn on earth
And see that each new wilful act
Alters the fibre of your being;
No learning becomes good and true
Until it changes the thing within.

CHANGE OF WEATHER

A brooding sky mantled with broken clouds
A bridge of shades arching the leafless bush.

She tiptoes through the clumps of yellow grass
And fires them up with a sparkle in her eye.

She had no time to talk; just smiled and went,
Leaving behind a trail of implied words.

This brought next morning a different kind of day.
Where the thick-leaved trees stood tall like temple towers
With bell-like blooms that a mad wind tinkle-tolled.
Raking a spot within your lower ribs
And making you see the world with altered eyes.

A dressed-up spider with black and yellow stripes
Swings up and down the angle of your door,
Winking in wicked glee and waiting there
For a guileless fly to come within its reach.

A bumblebee wheels around and hits the wall.
Then the wooden lintel before he finds the door.
But his whirling wings take him on a crazy ride
To the windowpane that knocks him to the floor.

Where he lifts his head and wobbles on spindly legs
To a sheltered corner to rest and start again.

This warms your blood. Bird-cries fill the air.
Doors fly open and make you wander out
And face a sky burning with warm desire.

MONSOON THOUGHTS

The rains are here today
With dark clouds and thunderbolts
In blustering panoply.
Winds lash the trees around.
Snake swirls of silver lightning
Spill out and slither down
The black sky to the blinking earth.

One such rainy afternoon
When day darkened to night,
Filled the house with shadows,
Wiped out the known details,
Turned it to a secret woodland,
We crept under the bed
And clung to each other
Neeli and I.

When I was ten and she was hardly nine—

Neeli's breath was hot
And smelt of milk and camphor
When she kissed me on the mouth
And with her probing fingers
Sketched out my body's map

And showed me the difference
Between her map and mine.

I was a witless dud,
She was the wiser one—
She knew the white and yellow
Of the egg of existence;

There were no more such rains
To bring us again together.
We grew up in different places.

I went to a boys' school
In a steamy seaside town.
She went to a fancy convent
In the cool of the Nilgiris.
Where a row of wimpled nuns
Groomed her to be a scholar
Concerned with the larger world.

I remained a wanderer,
Hopped from one thing to another
Never made a total run—
Comparing the diverse readings
Of the world you live within
And the world you visualized
I was always undecided—
Settled down to be an artist
And on the side scribble verses

Mixing their values up.
Looking for a speaking image
Searching for a coloured word.

Neeli saw some of these
Printed in a tiny booklet
In a shop in Nairobi
That sold art books and poems.
Mailed me a pretty card
With tiny bits of information
Of what she did and where.

She was going round and round
Various parts of Africa.
Meeting their villagers.
Making road maps for their progress.
Kissing their white-eyed kids,
Joking with giggling matrons,
Who flashed their beads and chintz
And smiles that shamed the moon.

Neeli wears gold-rimmed glasses
Her hair has now silver streaks.
She is surely close to fifty;
Doesn't look what she once was.

But her eyes have still the naughty glitter
That they had when she was nine,
Her nose is shapely, the ears are tender
And her smile still rings a bell.

My face is now criss-crossed with wrinkles
And caught within their puzzling maze,
My senses continue to search and wander
For a speaking shape or coloured word.

THE WALL

A crumbling wall with countless graffiti.
In bleeding reds and murky mud-washed blue.
Squirming squiggles, convoluted scrawls
Broad shadow smears with warped or weeping edge.

All teasing scripts of moments lost in time
Once full of breath and meaning, now worthless documents
Of ancient rivalries, of unquenched hates
Of hopes unfulfilled, of our ancient kin.

When we seek a site for building a new skyline
Of life untouched by the problems of the past
In an open space untainted by old fears,
Old frustrations and animosities,
This witless wall blocks up our horizons
And strews its detritus on our forward path.

Making us want to blast it out of sight.
And burn to ash its dark misleading signs.

But the pundits don't agree. They roll their eyes
Behind thick glasses washed with various hues.
Pull down this wall? Lose contact with our roots?
Which give our aspirations a sharp profile?

Forego our foothold, our hard-earned perch in time?
Oh, no! We need a sense of history.

The wall should remain. We will refill the gaps,
Repair the graffiti, revive their voice.
Enlarge the implication of their garbled signs.
And work out their total linkage A to Z.

And they succeed. They redraw the old divisions.
Rewrite the stories of old feuds and fights.
Archive their details. Display their tools
Graft the present on the exhumed past.
Re-fire the embers with issues long buried
And fill the air around with blinding smoke.

Now neighbours don't live in peace. They come to see
They were not friends but foes in days gone by
They feel ashamed—how could they forget that!
The scars and scabs embedded in their flesh?
Forsake their birthmarks and proud identities?

They no more greet or smile at each other.
Jab each other with eyes. Plan secret strategies
Of confrontation. Finally, take to arms,
Bash each others' heads, burn homes and properties.
And boast of these in loud fiendish glee.

The pundits rejoice—they have fresh work to do.
Survey the sights. Inventory the loss.

Analyse death and damage. Then speculate
On the wherefores and whys of what has come to be.

With probing eyes and protuberant nose
They seek to read the basic chemistry
Of their roots below. Societies' standing mores.
Their canons and customs. Their anthropology.
The cleavage lines of gender, class and caste.
The total plumbing of human existence.

And present their findings in enormous tomes
They heap upon and round the rebuilt wall
To augment its bulk, increase its towering height
And enlarge its shadow over a hapless land
Seeded with suspicion and crawling fears.

Then don their robes and say with a smirk or sigh,
The way things are, all these are bound to be.
The world is made that way. For all our polished looks
We hold within a venous undergrowth,
That muddles our hearts and misdirects our acts
Despite the passioned pleas of a Jesus Christ
A footloose Buddha. Nearer still, Gandhi.

A NEAR VISION

As the days pass by
And you gain in years
The past does not keep you captive.

You are born again each day
And the things you have seen for ages
Seem new to your virgin eyes
Each time you cross the street.

The dry leaves on the grassland
Dancing in the morning light;
The hedges edged with the laughter
Of windblown jasmine flowers;
The sky glowing blue and purple
Between the branching trees
Like the brilliant tessellations
Of ancient mosques and tombs.

Even the age-worn houses
Lining your neighbourhood
Seem like the grey denizens
Of an old forgotten land
With arches like broken dentures,
Doorways like patchwork quilts,
Windows curtained with shadows

Of long-lost history,
Walls soiled by peeling plaster
And coils of tangled wire
Supporting fancy hoardings
That advertise bras or bread.

But the roads look gay, the lamp posts
Sashay along its sides,
And shops decked with showy banners
Spill out with packaged goods
Thronging with men and women
In picturesque fancy dress;
Boys in their jeans and jerseys,
Girls in their miniskirts,
Seeming like they have stepped out
Of the doors of a fashion house.

All novel, holding no symptom
Of having been seen before.
So, you feel like leaning over
And asking the passers-by,
'Bhai, can you kindly tell me
The name of this pretty town?'

But having seen you daily
In this locality
They blink, smile and whisper softly
'This bald pate has lost his head.'

MAGIC OF MANTRAS

Sitting round the sacrificial fire
They are chanting sacred verses.
The sounds are smooth and deep
And their burden elevating;
Cloud-borne, starlit, wind-wafted
Floating high in the mind's measureless sky.

Speaking of origins and ends,
Body-hood and being,
Outer shells and inner convolutions,
Birth, decay and death
And the endless circulation
Of the cyclic stream of life.

The sound is mesmerizing—
Wipes out the ache in the limbs,
The burning in the belly,
The rattling tumult in the restless mind
Battling the pros and cons of everything;
Of missed goals and messed-up chances,
Ambitions unfulfilled.

That is when a monkey lands on the roof
And brings down a mouldy rafter,
Shatters the canopy of peace,

Calls back the previous scene,
Rolls in the web of shadows,
Restarts the weary chase,
In the cramped meandering street
That runs from nowhere to nowhere.

This brings back the pain in the leg,
The ache in the stomach
And the whole scene of doubts and discomforts
Instils a howling vacancy
In the bone-pit of your chest.

THE MYNA OF MYNAMATI

The myna came and sat upon the side
Of the windowsill—put out one yellow foot
Then advanced the other; opened its brown beak wide
And uttered a friendly squeak. With eyes black as soot
Goggled with yellow, it looked up and scanned my face.
May I have a word with you dear sir, he said.
I replied, Certainly, though I am a bit amazed
That you sound like a human being well born and bred.
That is thanks to a new device we are equipped with,
Straight from the time we hatch. I speak English to you.
To Pierre next door and his petite friend Edith
I speak polished French. I can speak German too.
And various other tongues. Mynas now descry
Your past and the future too with an inner eye.

Good gracious me! I said to myself
There is nothing now you can store in your inner shelf.

Do you recall when you were a student here
You knew one of my handsome ancestors?
I surely did. His eyes ran ear to ear.
He had an orange beak. His voice was hoarse
Like a husky Hollywood star's. He greeted you
With a chuckle; then chanted loud and clear

Radha Krishna kaho. I had no clue
How he managed this. By practice sheer?
Or through an inborn gift? Shit! Said my friend
He was trained for this by a round of cuffs and kicks
Which ruined his health and killed him in the end.
We have no more of this. Even when we are chicks
We carry within our heads some microchips
That make us linguists without apprenticeship.

Sometimes these chips cross-link and give us powers
They were not meant to do. Like new insights
That unzip easily the outer covers
Of things long past, even foreview unborn sites.
Of our own selves and others we come across.
That is how I know you know my ancestor
I can also tell you all things that came to pass
In your bygone days. And what is more
Give you a glimpse of what is yet to be—
Hold it! I said, Keep all that in your mind.
What is past is past. And I don't want to see
What is on the date pad before I myself find
What I can do to steer it in my way,
Not run on rails prelaid a previous day.

I will not let any bird or priest or pope
Insert their views into my horoscope

The myna blinked, opened its shining beak
To say something. I stopped him with a sign.

You are smart my dear but this clairvoyant streak
May not always carry if the subject does not deign
To take things as they come. Life is an onward flow
That freezes when the date-stamp strikes it down;
But stamp to stamp it can manage to grow
Outside the settled codes, quite unbeknown—
The known is a burden, the unknown an open sky
You can conquer with your wings as you birds
    know well.
The myna laughs, You are surely a funny guy.
Others flatter me to hear their own death knell
Then sigh and sink and take things as they come
But here you are, beating your battle drum.

Though I am delighted, adds the bright-eyed bird,
Life is more fun when you can rescript it
And change the action plan, if not word by word,
Free it a bit from the grip of the ancient writ.
I can sell you a work-plan (if you will like to buy)
To achieve this. Our man-management cell
Can fix things up and make you own the sky
Of endless innovation—just ring the bell
Under the knob-like thorn of that simul tree.
We sit in conference on its topmost bough
All graduate MBS of Mynamati.
Then he puffed his chest to look like a wise old crow,
It won't cost you much, just a piece of candied fruit
Which helps to keep us trim from crest to foot.

CHANGE OF SCENE

There is a kind of alchemy in love
That redoes the look of things you see around,
Turns spills of gloomy slag to shining gold
And greens the grimy earth.

Transforms a fleabag town into a fairyland
A slummy city into a shining carnival
Where even ageing girls look elves and dreary men
The dressed-up members of a pantheon.

Where crossing the road you feel as tall as trees
Making you stoop to save your crazy head
From hitting the doorjamb of the lowering sky.
Where the breeze drives you silly and the bead-eyed birds
Warble and say, You too have inborn wings
You can open out and cross the hedge of clouds.
Into an endless sky. And float from star to star
Where your unborn dreams find space to sprout and bloom.

And out in the fields you hug the crackled trees
Like they are long-lost friends, as also the sky-high palms
With body rings straight from the root to neck
And the grass tickling your foot says, Lay it soft
I hold a tiny shoot between two blades
That seeks to kiss your feet.

And a bearded goat looks up and winks at you.
Bleats out a greeting you think you understand,
Bravo, young friend! Your day has started well.
Then out in the river that has broken into pools
You see a message the sunbeams have pencilled in
This day will last as long as you both last.

REMINISCENCE

The soap-case stares at you like a lidless eye.
A smell of sandal survives on its rims.

The clothes on the racks softened by frequent use
Speak of the body they once held within
With a whiff of jasmine and a trace of sweat

The much-read books are splitting at the ribs
Their page-ends curling up like pouting lips

The sunken cushion upon the vacant chair
Holds tell-tale folds and frayed and gaping seams

The unworn socks thrust into old footwear
Lie here and there below the empty bed.

The absence storms the silence of your chest,
Raising old sounds, reviving time-lost words
Setting afloat the shadows of the past
In the surrounding air.

You have to go some time,
She often said
And in the state I am
I feel the time has come

Then looking at the bush of lilies near the hedge
Like a host of children waving tiny flags.

These voiceless things hold you
And make you stay
And seem to say, If you still have to go
Do so another day.

But that day came
Much faster than I thought.

PASSAGE

There is nothing to tell
The story has ended.
The vacant days and nights
Pass like a line of ants
Crawling from one hole to another,
From a crack in the window ledge
To a slit on the chequered floor,
Carrying a load of eggs
Raised high above their heads.

What do they hold within?
The meat of an unborn future?
The map of a sudden end?

AFTER MALEGAON

You do not have to go
To anatomy rooms
To see dismembered bodies

You can see them on the street.

Eyes blown out of sockets,
Faces ripped apart,
Torsos crushed and mangled,
Torn limbs strewn around,
Like playthings in the pathways
For stray dogs to tug and tear.

Streets are now open playfields
For wild men on the prowl
Masked out of identity
With black dress, hood and gloves
Seeking to blast the bodies
Of unwarned fellow beings.

To assert a waning manhood?
To express an inner hurt?
To avenge an ancient grievance,
Or serve a faceless god
Made out of stone or timber
Or a non-material myth

Born out of countless stories
That spew from many mouths
Where each new wash of spittle
Reshapes a previous tale
Painting in shadow patches
That lead one's mind astray
Cloud it with dark suspicions
Seed it with barbs of hate.

Streets no more ring with laughter
Doors stare like vacant eyes
Hold whispers in shaded corners
Wails in the corridors.

The wails are warped with anger
Tears hiss like molten lead
The heart's once smiling garden
Is a patch of deadened earth
Spewing new bugs of hatred
In each human, beast or thing
Cramping their growth and action
Shrinking their inner selves.

Trees chop the sky like hatchets,
Grass flares like blown-up fire,
Birds slash the air with curses,
Beasts glare with gory eyes
And each man sees his neighbour
A monster in human dress.

HOMOPOLIS

You think you are a person
With a mint-marked face and body
A singular gait and speech
A foolproof fingerprint
A prefigured DNA.

So dress up and smile for a snapshot
For others to see and say
This is surely so-and-so

But some think you are a mansion
Even larger, a row-house street.

Housing a million microbes
Unseen by normal eyes
That control your inner traffic
From wherever they sit,
Switch on your pangs of hunger,
Sweep in the swallowed food,
Soak it in steamy juices,
Turn it into flowing blood,
Run it through throbbing channels,
To a secret central pool.

Some help;
But some are harmful;
Some build;
But some unbuild
The streets of this homopolis.
Do all this under cover.
The snapshots can't locate them,
Unless they screen and scan
With all kinds of new devices
And read out the cryptic codes
That reel off their ticking ends.

Even in your normal viewing
You are not wholly you.

When in the early morning
You go to wash your head
Before a laughing mirror,
Good Lord! You notice there
Your eyes move quite freely
On the floor-mat of your face
Wink, blink, stare and ogle,
Shoot slanting glances,
Squint,
Quake soft like trembling jelly,
Freeze hard like sharp-edged flint
To say, though we are within you
You are part of what we see.

Then, when your jaws fall open
And show you your shadowed mouth
You see with wide-eyed wonder
Your ribbed and restless tongue
That unfolds its fleshy body
Like a squirming caged-in beast
Or swims in a pool of spittle,
A playful skin-robed squid,
Greets you with handless gesture,
Watches with eyeless stare
And runs its grainy edges
Upon the lips and teeth;
Rears up like a rising reptile
To the rooftop of your mouth.
Seeming quite independent.
A visitor from outer space?
A loose-limbed sleek alien
Who sneaked in a previous night
When you left your lip-door open
And the fencing of your teeth
While groping in sleep-sunk waters
For the white buds of your dreams?

SPEAKING OF OLD DAYS

They came here they say
When the trains were few
And the station was a brick-built cabin.
And the pebbly earth around
Glistened bloody red
Fissured by sun,
Furrowed by monsoon showers;
Where a late day wind
Loosened the leaves from the trees
And rolled them on the ground,
Raising in the silent air
The sounds of a busy street,
A mad, intriguing mix
Of garbled conversation,
Guffaws of laughter,
Whistles and whispers
And squirts of exclamations.

And when the wind stopped,
The sky was a sheet of silence
Pinned tight in the four directions
By the cries of whining kites.

THE SHADOW

When I undid the latch
And peeped out to see who knocked,
I saw nobody there,
Only a shadow patch
Near the open door,
Flat on the shining floor
Which raised its fissured rims
To say it was moving in.

I let it, with a nod.
You can't shut shadows out
When they seek to come inside,
Can't sweep them out with a broom,
Scrub them out with a brush,
Wipe them out with a mop.
They always come on top.

Quickly the shadow moved
And snaked into the corner spots.

Then a neighbour's record player
Started playing a mournful tune,
The call of a lonesome maid
For her lover to come back soon.
A ghazal of the common kind

Which soured up in the space around
And curdled the limpid air.

This summoned the shadows out,
Spread them on the floor and wall,
A thin layer of murky grey,
Like you see in an unwashed sink,
Which soon grew dark and thick
To depth of blue-black ink
Wiping out the glowing whites,
Fogging up the blinking lights.

In this sweep of black and blue
I started missing Sue.

THE NIGHT AT RISHIKESH

Bells from the distant temples,
Shouts from the night-sogged streets,
The odour of mango blossom,
Incense from the river front.

They are flat on the milky terrace
In the sight of a million stars.

Her body shone like the silver
Of a newly landed fish,
Eyes rimmed with fear and longing,
Mouth split with an unspelt wish.

His mind was asking itself,
Standing on unsure toes,
Can one possess this body
That glows like a cloud in the sky?
Touch it with uncouth fingers,
Fold it in calloused arms,
Peel down its silken glamour,
Soak it in the body's sweat,
Seek inside its shining halo,
A dark spot to hide his head?

Just then both heard a whisper
In the pit of their doubting heads;
Close tight your eyes you fatheads
Respond to the call of flesh;
Sight is a ruthless censor,
Stiffens your throbbing nerves,
Strangles your resolution,
Stifles your inner cry.

That is when the jousting started
Between the angel and the eyeless beast,
One clad in the sky's high colours,
The other dyed in the earth's deep red.
Blind gropings in the vaulted tunnels.
Steep climbs in the open skies,
For the price of a fleeting moment
On the cloud-capped mountain peak,
Then the fall in a whistling descent
To the floor of a waveless deep.

TO SOMNATH ZUTSHI

A self-appointed cop
Out on a random beat
In the media street.
Bristling with news of coups
Crises and calumnies;
And ways some human beings
Bring misery to their own kind,
And transform this shining planet
Into a misbegotten slum.

Much more so in our quarter
Whose young men sit and sleep
Hire Gods to do their bidding
Buying them with gifts and gold.

No wonder you came each morning,
Blowing your (balding) top,
After seeing in the morning papers,
Something to shout about,
Of the odd men in the larger world
Or those in your neighbourhood,
Brainless rulers, spineless youth,
Dissolute priests and holy men,
Leaders who think they have changed the world.

By painting red railings blue and green.
NGOs who did social work
As a covered means to serve themselves,
Liars! play actors, petty thieves,
Wearing the robes of lofty saints,
All things that set your mind ablaze
And give your speech a caustic edge.

I shall miss you friend when I no more get
To see you when I come to town
And hear your views
On the latest news
With the usual heat
And rhetoric.

SHADOW WORLD

I now live within
A curious interweave
Of sleep and wakefulness.
A sleep streaked with the shining threads
Of rekindled strands of life.
A wakefulness that swims within
A loaded lotus pond of dreams,
With half-open buds, humming bees,
Tadpoles that flick their glossy tails
And scatter tiny spots of light
In the shadows underneath.
This removed the marking stones
Between what is and what you see,
Between the seen thing and the sign.
We communicate from Skype to Skype
From one shade to another shade.